MW00756061

LOSERTHiNK

PORTFOLIO / PENGUIN

LOSERTHiNK

How Untrained Brains Are Ruining America

SCOTT ADAMS

PORTFOLIO/PENGUIN
An imprint of Penguin Random House LLC
penguinrandomhouse.com

Copyright © 2019 by Scott Adams, Inc.
Illustrations copyright © 2019 by Scott Adams, Inc.
Penguin supports copyright. Copyright fuels creativity, encourages diverse voices, promotes free speech, and creates a vibrant culture. Thank you for buying an authorized edition of this book and for complying with copyright laws by not reproducing, scanning, or distributing any part of it in any form without permission. You are supporting writers and allowing Penguin to continue to publish books for every reader.

Most Portfolio books are available at a discount when purchased in quantity for sales promotions or corporate use. Special editions, which include personalized covers, excerpts, and corporate imprints, can be created when purchased in large quantities. For more information, please call (212) 572-2232 or e-mail specialmarkets@penguinrandomhouse .com. Your local bookstore can also assist with discounted bulk purchases using the Penguin Random House corporate Business-to-Business program. For assistance in locating a participating retailer, e-mail B2B@penguinrandomhouse.com.

Library of Congress Cataloging-in-Publication Data
Names: Adams, Scott, 1957– author.
Title: Loserthink : how untrained brains are ruining America / Scott Adams.
Description: New York : Portfolio/Penguin, 2019. |
Includes bibliographical references and index. |
Identifiers: LCCN 2019022926 (print) | LCCN 2019022927 (ebook) |
ISBN 9780593083529 (hardcover) | ISBN 9780593083536 (ebook)
ISBN 9780593086339 (international edition)
Subjects: LCSH: Thought and thinking. | Divergent thinking. | Reasoning.
Classification: LCC BF441 .A285 2019 (print) | LCC BF441 (ebook) | DDC 153.4/2—dc23
LC record available at https://lccn.loc.gov/2019022926
LC ebook record available at https://lccn.loc.gov/2019022927

Printed in the United States of America
1   3   5   7   9   10   8   6   4   2

BOOK DESIGN BY ELLEN CIPRIANO

Penguin is committed to publishing works of quality and integrity. In that spirit, we are proud to offer this book to our readers; however, the story, the experiences, and the words are the author's alone.

For my love, Kristina

Contents

LOSERTHiNK

CHAPTER 1

What Is Loserthink?

Despite evidence to the contrary, we all use our brains. But most of us have never learned how to think effectively. I'm not talking about IQ or other measures of intelligence, which matter in their own way, of course. I'm talking about thinking as a learned skill. We don't teach thinking in schools, and you can see the results of that nearly every day. If you use social media, or you make the mistake of paying attention to other people's opinions in any form, you're probably seeing a lot of absurd and unproductive reasoning that I call *loserthink*.

Loserthink isn't about being dumb, and it isn't about being underinformed. Loserthink is about *unproductive* ways of thinking. You can be smart and well informed while at the same time being a flagrant loserthinker. That is not only possible; it's the normal situation. My observation, after several decades on this planet, is that clear thinking is somewhat rare. And there's a reason for that. No matter how smart you are, if you don't have experience across multiple domains, you're probably not equipped with the most productive ways of thinking.

> Loserthink isn't about being dumb, and it isn't about being under-informed. Loserthink is about unproductive ways of thinking.

For example, a trained engineer learns a certain way of thinking about the world that overlaps but is different from how a lawyer, a philosopher, or an economist thinks. Having any one of those skill sets puts you way ahead in understanding the world and thinking about it productively. But unless you have sampled the thinking techniques across different fields, you are missing a lot. And again, to be super clear, I am not talking about the facts one learns in those disciplines. I am only talking about the *techniques of thinking* that students of those fields pick up during the process of learning.

The good news is that you don't need to master the fields of engineering, science, economics, philosophy, law, or any other field in order to learn the basics of how to think the way experts in those areas think. For example, if you didn't know what the concept of *sunk costs* is all about, I could explain it in thirty seconds and you would fully understand it.

Sunk costs: Money you already spent shouldn't influence your
decision about what to do next, but for psychological reasons,
it often does.

I wrote this book to get you acquainted with (or remind you of) the most productive thinking techniques borrowed from multiple domains. Collectively, they will help you avoid unproductive loserthink.

Tiger Woods was born with a lucky arrangement of DNA that allowed him to dominate the game of golf for years. But his natural talents would have been wasted had he not learned the strategies and techniques of golf. This is true of any learned behavior. Natural talent can only get you so far. If you want to be good at the not-so-ordinary task of thinking productively, you need to learn some techniques and then practice them. Your so-called common sense can dupe you into believing you already know how to think effectively.[1]

I'll show you what you might be missing.

Expect to read in this book some ideas that you already know, plus some things you don't. Everyone is coming to this book from a different starting point. I know from experience that many of you will give this book as a gift to the unproductive thinkers in your lives, and I wanted to create a complete picture for them, if not for you, O wise book-giver. I'm guessing that half of the people reading this book already knew how to think about sunk costs the right way. The other half just caught up.

Learning how to think productively does not come naturally to any of us. But it is easy to learn. You simply have to be exposed to the techniques and you'll likely remember them for the rest of your life. The techniques are simple to understand and easy to master. This book will set your brain filters to recognize loserthink wherever you encounter it, in others and in yourself.

We humans give greater weight to things that have names. And giving loserthink its name creates a shorthand way of mocking people who practice unproductive thinking. Mockery gets a bad rap, but I think we can agree it can be useful when intelligently applied. For example, mocking people for lying probably helps to reduce future lies and make the world a better place, whereas mocking people for things they can't change is just being a jerk.

As the creator of the Dilbert comic strip, I use mockery almost every day to keep the most ridiculous management practices from spreading.

If that sounds like I have an exaggerated sense of my impact on society, consider that, in 2018, Tesla CEO Elon Musk wrote a memo to all employees in which he explained how to be productive in meetings. Here is one of his rules.

> Elon Musk's Rule Six: "In general, always pick common sense as your guide. If following a 'company rule' is obviously ridiculous in a particular situation, such that it would make for a great *Dilbert* cartoon, then the rule should change."

Notice that it was easier for Musk to describe what he wanted of his employees because the word *Dilbert* exists in their common vocabulary and they all have a sense of what a *Dilbert*-like policy looks like. Naming things can weaponize them.

I used the Tesla example because it was easy to find a published quote. But I can tell you that for almost three decades I have been getting direct reports from managers of big companies telling me they changed or avoided policies because "We don't want to end up in a *Dilbert* comic," or words to that effect. The risk of mockery changes behavior. I would go so far as to say it is one of history's most powerful forces.

If you have a negative word for something, it's easier to avoid it than if you don't. Before I introduced the term *loserthink*, what word would you have used to describe a smart person who has a mental blind spot caused by a lack of exposure across different fields? You would probably default to the closest word in your vocabulary, which might be *stupid, dumb, idiot,* and the like. I don't have to tell you it's hard to change someone's mind after you call him an idiot. And if you take the high road and the intellectual path, describing a person's mental blind spots with terms such as *confirmation bias* or *cognitive dissonance,* your target will claim you are actually the one suffering from those cognitive errors, and the discussion goes nowhere.

> If you have a negative word for something, it will be easier to avoid it than if you don't.

Now compare those useless approaches to what I am offering you here. You have my permission to take a photo of any individual page in this book and share it on social media, or with people you know, as your response to any situation in which you identify loserthink. The fact that the page will come from a published book adds weight to your point and depersonalizes the conversation so it doesn't seem like your own crazy opinion. If you describe the copied page as coming from the book Loserthink, you have both mockery and unearned credibility on your side. And when this book becomes a bestseller, it will gain even more power as a suppressor of loserthink.

By now you might be wondering why I counsel against calling people stupid while at the same time I introduce the word loserthink, which seems just as bad. The difference is that stupid refers to a person whereas loserthink applies to the technique. And keep in mind that all of us engage in loserthink sometimes. The loser part of loserthink refers to the outcome, not the DNA of the person involved. Remember to make that distinction if you use the term. Calling people stupid will not make them turn smart, but pointing out a bad technique and contrasting it with a good one can, in time, move people to a more productive way of thinking. As with my example of sunk costs, once you are exposed to the concept for the first time, it almost automatically becomes part of your future thinking.

I'm only able to write this book because I have made most of the mistakes I describe in these pages. I've learned from experience how to recognize those errors in myself and in others. In too many cases, I learned these techniques after being mocked by credible people (*ouch!*). None of us is exempt from occasional loserthink, but I hope what you read here will help you avoid the mockery I experienced over the years while unintentionally learning how to write this book.

Loserthink also serves as an explanation for why Hollywood artists seem—at least to many of us—more sincere than smart when they speak out on political or social issues. You aren't imagining that something strange is going on there. Most people in the entertainment industry are not trained scientists, engineers, lawyers, economists, philosophers, or knowledgeable in any of the fields in which decision-making is taught. Adding to this effect is that, as human beings, we *don't know what we don't know.* If you have never been exposed to lessons on how to think effectively, you wouldn't have a frame of reference to know whether or not you were doing it right.

You might be a naturally bright person, which seems likely because you are reading this book. And perhaps you once took a logic class. That would be a great start, but it wouldn't help you see the world the way people who have studied other disciplines see it. If you have been exposed to the thinking styles of only a few disciplines—let's say history and philosophy—you would still have gaps in terms of understanding how economists and scientists see the world.

If you have been exposed to the thinking styles of only a few disciplines, you will have large gaps in your ability to productively think about the world.

For example, you might know Seth MacFarlane as the creator of the hugely successful animated TV show Family Guy, but that's a sliver of his accomplishments. He has one of the most impressive stacks of world-class talent you will ever see in one human being. He's a singer, actor, writer, artist, producer, humorist, and voice talent. But does that tell us MacFarlane has the right combination of education and experiences to understand our world? Would that set of thinking skills (the ones we know about) compare favorably to a person with deep experience across the domains of science, business, and psychology, for example? Based on MacFarlane's extraordinary success, it appears he is talented in all of the fields in which he has succeeded. My impression from afar is that his natural intelligence (IQ) is extraordinarily high. He graduated from the Rhode Island School of Design and has racked up one success after another in various entertainment domains (animation, movies, live-action TV, music, award show hosting, etc.) while making new fortunes from almost every one of them. In other words, he's a super-smart guy. And I have no reason to doubt his good intentions.

That said, based on his Twitter comments about politics, it does not appear that he has much experience with the fields of study that teach us how best to think about our world. If that describes you as well, you wouldn't notice anything was missing from MacFarlane's political opinions or your own. I'll give you one good example to make my point. In the following tweet, MacFarlane is saying, in effect, that we can be sure climate change is real and dangerous because of the massive number of scientists who say so.

If your experience in life has been concentrated in the arts, it would seem entirely reasonable to rely on the consensus of climate science experts. And if you observed that others were not doing the same, you might conclude that those folks are morons who can't see the obvious.

I can't read Seth MacFarlane's mind, but his tweet seems to communicate something along those lines.

Now let's say you had experience in economics and business, as I do. In those domains, anyone telling you they can predict the future in ten years with their complicated multivariate models is automatically considered a fraud. History is littered with people who had prediction models for picking stocks. When lots of people are making lots of predictions about the future, some of them are guaranteed to be closer than others. And those people will advertise their powers to divine the future so they can rope in customers who don't understand that professional investment advice is largely a legal form of fraud. I have a degree in economics and an MBA from a top business school, plus years of personal investing experience, so I'm not guessing on this topic. Anyone with my experience would tell you that most (but not all) financial advice, in terms of picking individual stocks, is bunk. And yet there is an industry full of financial experts who do exactly that and charge large amounts for it. If you asked them how valid their methods were, they would tell you they don't get it right every time, but on average they are adding a lot of value.

Similarly, the field of climate science is a perfect breeding ground for confirmation bias, cognitive dissonance, and outright fraud. That doesn't mean climate scientists are wrong or dishonest, and I make no such claim. But it does mean it would be sensible to dial down your sense of certainty about their rightness.

You might be debating me in your mind right now and thinking that, unlike the field of finance, the scientific process drives out bias over time. Studies are peer reviewed, and experiments that can't be reproduced are discarded.

Is that what is happening?

Here I draw upon my sixteen years working in corporate America. If my job involved reviewing a complicated paper from a peer, how much checking of the data and the math would I do when I am already overworked? Would I travel to the original measuring instruments all over the world and check their calibrations? Would I compare the raw data to the "adjusted" data that is used in the paper? Would I do a deep dive on the math and reasoning, or would I skim it for obvious mistakes? Unless scientists are a different kind of human being than the rest of us, they would intelligently cut corners whenever they think they could get away with it, just like everyone else. Assuming scientists are human, you would expect lots of peer-reviewed studies to be flawed. And that turns out to be the situation. As the New York Times reported in 2018, the peer review process is defective to the point of being laughable.[2]

Thousands of climate scientists agree with the idea that the planet is warming in an unprecedented way. But how many of those scientists are directly involved in measuring temperatures versus how many are simply relying on the data from a smaller group that does that work?

While it is relatively easy to know if a certain region is warm compared to recent decades, one must rely on historical data to know how unusual that is in terms of the earth's history. How many scientists in the world do you imagine have worked directly on determining historical proxy temperature measurements, such as tree rings and ice cores? A handful? A thousand? I have no idea. And neither do you.

Based on my experience in corporate America, I'm biased toward thinking only a handful of scientists worldwide have top-level direct experience estimating global temperature measurements for years prior to 1979 and the satellite era. And that group of scientists, however large or small it is, seems to control the foundational argument that our current warming rate is unprecedented and human-caused.

Based on my life of experience across multiple fields, and especially with large organizations, I'll bet no more than a handful of people in the world are true experts in measuring global temperatures. And given that the ocean controls something like 90 percent of the heat retention on the planet, do you believe we can measure the average ocean temperatures, both now and in our far distant history, to a precision necessary to know if a few degrees up or down have happened before, and at what rate? Maybe we can. I can't rule it out. I'll just say it doesn't pass my sniff test, but I acknowledge that my sniffing is not science. I'd like to be wrong and learn that scientists can measure to that level of accuracy.

I have been researching climate science claims for a few months to see if I could arrive at a rational opinion on my own, and I see the following pattern over and over:

> CLIMATE SCIENTIST: Here's my chart using official and publicly available temperature data proving the planet is warming at an alarming rate.
>
> SKEPTIC: Here's my chart using official and publicly available temperature data showing you are wrong, and here's why . . .
>
> CLIMATE SCIENTIST: Here's a paper showing why the way you are charting things is incorrect.
>
> SKEPTIC: Here's a logical argument showing you why that paper is wrong.
>
> CLIMATE SCIENTIST: Oh, yeah? Well, here's my logical argument for why your logical argument is wrong.

And so on to infinity.

In theory, a nonscientist should be able to follow the climate debate to its conclusion and judge whether the scientists or the skeptics have the best argument. But in reality, all one can do is chase the arguments back and forth until one of the players says something scientific that you don't understand. Then, if you are like most normal adults, you default to believing whichever side you already thought was right. The topic of climate science is effectively impenetrable for nonscientists.

Consider the skeptical argument about the alleged "seventeen-year pause" in warming from 1996 to 2014 that NASA satellites measured. Skeptics say the pause disproves human-driven climate change because CO_2 was rising sharply in that time while temperatures were not. Climate scientists counter that criticism by saying you can't draw any conclusions from looking at a "cherry-picked" period less than thirty years in duration because short-term natural variations can mask the CO_2-caused warming that is happening on average over the long term. But climate scientists also tell us that our most recent thirty years are showing warming that is highly meaningful. How can both things be true? Thirty years of temperature data either tells you something useful or it doesn't. I assume the real problem here is my personal ignorance, and not necessarily a problem with climate science. I assume climate scientists have a good response to the alleged temperature pause, but I wouldn't understand it if I heard it. My point is that a concerned citizen is largely helpless in trying to understand how settled the science of climate change really is. But that doesn't stop us from having firm opinions on the topic. Ask Seth MacFarlane.

If you have no experience in the field of science, you might think the climate models created by scientists are "science" because scientists make them. But prediction models are not science. They are an intelligent combination of scientific thinking, math, human judgment, and incomplete data. That's why there are lots of different climate models, all a bit different.

If you have not studied the methods of magicians and scam artists, you might not recognize that climate forecast models fit a common scam model. The scam works by sending thousands of emails with, let's say, three different stock predictions to random people while claiming your proprietary algorithm says those stocks will rise. If any one of the three stocks goes up, entirely by chance, the group that got that particular stock recommendation will think the algorithm works. Then the scammer sends another batch of three different stock predictions to subsets of the group that got the lucky guesses from the first round.

By chance, a few people in the second group might receive stock recommendations that performed well for no predictable reason. Now they think the algorithm is two-for-two in success. By the third round of this scam, the few people who ended up with three amazing stock predictions, completely by chance, will send the scammers a large check to invest on their behalf. After all, what are the odds of three stock predictions in a row being so accurate? The scam works because the targets of the scam don't see any of the predictions that were wrong, so they lack important context.

Similar to the stock scam, climate scientists discard climate models that don't fit with observations. The public doesn't hear about the models that are discarded. If you start with hundreds of different predictions, and you discard the ones that miss their initial predictions, you are nearly guaranteed to end up with some models that *seem* to predict the future, but only by chance.

Did you know that?

If all you know is how many times someone hit a target, it is loserthink to judge how accurate they are. You also need to know how many times they missed.

If you were already aware that climate models are not science, and that they fit the pattern of well-known scams (sometimes called marketing), and that it is fairly normal for the consensus of scientists to be dead wrong, you probably have a healthy skepticism about climate predictions of doom.

One thing I can say with complete certainty is that it is a bad idea to trust the majority of experts in any domain in which both complexity and large amounts of money are involved. You end up with this:

Well, yes, our predictions were completely wrong, but now we know why they were wrong. If you give us a million dollars to fix it, our predictions will be accurate from this point on. Don't ask me what we fixed or how we did it because you wouldn't understand. It's complicated.

Whenever you have a lot of money in play, combined with the

ability to hide misbehavior behind complexity, you should expect widespread fraud to happen. Take, for example, the 2019 Duke University settlement in which the university agreed to pay $112.5 million for repeatedly submitting research grant requests with falsified data. Duke had a lot of grant money at stake, and lots of complexity in which to hide bad behavior. Fraud was nearly guaranteed.[3]

> When lots of money and lots of complexity are in play, fraud is nearly guaranteed.

If you have been on this planet for a long time, as I have, and you pay attention to science, you know that the consensus of scientists on the topic of nutrition was wrong for decades. The most striking example of that involved the introduction of the USDA's food guide pyramid in 1992, which recommended that consumers eat more bread, cereal, rice, and pasta than vegetables and fruits. That is opposite what nutrition experts recommend today. Critics make a compelling case that the food industry influenced nutrition science and the USDA's recommendations to the point of making nutrition "science" a complete joke. But it was a joke the public thought was science until we learned it wasn't.[4]

Personally, I believed what nutrition scientists were saying in the nineties—so much so that I started a food company dedicated to making the most nutritious food item possible, using science as my guide. I called it the Dilberito, and it was fortified with all of the vitamins and minerals the government said you needed, based on science, I thought. The Dilberito also had a good ratio of protein to carbs. Sounds great, right? The problem, which I learned the hard way, was that what the experts "knew" about nutrition kept changing. Over time, it became painfully obvious to me that nutrition science wasn't science at all. It was some unholy marriage of industry influence, junk science, and government. Any one of those things is bad, but when you put those three forces together, people die. That isn't hyperbole. Bad nutrition science has probably killed a lot of people in the past few decades.[5]

Scientists were wrong when they predicted we had already reached so-called peak oil. Scientists were wrong about the ozone layer being beyond repair (the hole is shrinking).[6] Experts were wrong that the year 2000 computer bug would crash computer systems worldwide (it got fixed in time). But if I am being fair, those problems probably got solved because we panicked about them ahead of time. A little bit of creative panic goes a long way.[7]

If you have studied psychology and economics, you would understand that the overwhelming consensus of climate scientists could easily be more wrong than right, and it wouldn't be unusual in human history. Whenever you have money, reputations, power, ego, and complexity in play, it is irrational to assume you are seeing objective science. The fields of psychology and economics have shown us in a thousand ways that people are influenced by all sorts of forces while generally not being aware of how much they are being biased. In other words, the only way one could be dead certain that the consensus of scientists is right on any topic that can't be replicated in a controlled experiment, or proven true by math, is by ignoring the entire fields of psychology, economics, history, and—if you are older—your own experience.

On top of that, if you also have a background in business and economics, you might understand that, in the face of unknown risks, it is wise to keep your economy humming at maximum strength in case you later need to make an expensive push to scrub the CO_2 out of the air (which is already possible but insanely expensive) or perhaps to fix whatever the climate breaks.

If you have a background in economics and business, you might recognize that the cost of scrubbing CO_2 from the air—should we ever need to do so—will likely drop in cost every year with new technology. And that means that waiting a few years to get serious on funding CO_2 air-scrubbers is likely the smarter play than going hard at it now when the technology is super expensive and less efficient than future versions are likely to be. Starting later could easily get you to the point you want sooner and cheaper.

A good example of this dynamic is my investment in solar panels for my home a decade ago. If I had waited three years to install the solar panels on my roof, taking advantage of the falling cost and higher efficiency of newer units, I would have saved money and ended up with a system that was better for the environment in the long run. I understood that dynamic when I made the decision, but I installed the solar panels anyway for a variety of social reasons. In California, if you have a new home and no solar panels, it's a bad look.

When scientists say human activity increases the rate of climate warming, I take it seriously. The basic science around climate change (chemistry and physics, for example) is likely to be more reliable than the prediction models. I only object to arguments that say the consensus of scientists agree with the prediction models, and therefore so should you. The prediction models are more about persuasion than science. I don't object to well-intentioned persuasion, so long as it is for the common good.

Climate scientists might be 100 percent right when they say the planet is warming at a dangerous rate and that CO_2 is the main driver. I am not qualified to check their work. But I am qualified to say that *the way climate science is presented to the public* is not credible to people who have *my type of experience*, even if it turns out that most climate scientists are right.

I don't intend to change your mind about climate change. I haven't even made up my own mind, and perhaps I never will, given the difficulty in mastering the topic. The point is to show you how your experience, and therefore your filters on a topic, can get you to very different opinions compared to other smart people using the same set of facts. Does your opinion of climate change look a lot like mine, or is it closer to MacFarlane's view that it makes sense to follow the consensus of experts? My hope is that you can now look at the topic of climate change through more than one filter. For many of you, this will be the first time you can do that. Some of you were already there.

When you are done with this book, you will be equipped to go beyond calling a suboptimal argument stupid/idiotic/moronic and the like. You'll be able to identify loserthink wherever you see it, and you will be able to point to relevant chapters in this book when you want to flag an example of it in others. You'll be amazed how well that works compared to insulting people's intelligence.

In the first part of this book, I will introduce you to the most useful thinking patterns from a variety of disciplines. I'll stick with the ideas that have direct use in your daily life, not the exotic theories and math. Once you have that grounding, I'll teach you how to identify your own mental prison walls and push through them. And finally, I'll teach you how to help others out of their mental prisons.

Mental prison: The illusions and unproductive thinking that limit our ability to see the world clearly and act upon it rationally.

MY QUALIFICATIONS

What makes me qualified to help people think more productively?

That's a fair question. I think you deserve an answer before you go much further in this book.

You probably know I'm the creator of the Dilbert comic strip, which is one of the most successful comic strips in history. I make fun of the jargon-talkers, the fad-believers, and the bull****ers in every workplace. People have been telling me for years that I helped them see past management pseudoscience and other ridiculous beliefs that infect the workplace. With Dilbert, my primary tools for helping readers escape their mental prisons are humor and mockery.

I learned years ago that it is nearly impossible to mock a *good* idea unless you also lie about its nature or leave out important context. Mockery only succeeds in persuading against absurd beliefs—the kind that form mental prison walls. If I can make you laugh at your situation, I'm probably helping you see your mental prison walls more clearly.

I am also a trained hypnotist, and I have studied and written on the topic of persuasion for decades. My prior book, *Win Bigly*, is entirely about persuasion. I have been using a persuasion skill set for most of my adult life to help people see the world more clearly. And I know from experience that doing so isn't a task the untrained can do. Your smart friends don't have the right tools and techniques to get out of their mental prisons, and there's a good chance that describes you as well. The business models of the press and social media act in concert to keep you in your mental prison, like some sort of indentured servant working on a click farm. As long as you are clicking on the media's content, that's all they need from you. And they know you'll click with more passion if they can keep you spinning around in your biased bubble.

There is no job title called Mental Prison Escape Consultant. If you have an actual mental health problem, doctors and therapists can help. But they won't help you know how wrong you are about the everyday fabric of reality. Your doctor can't cure you from watching biased news sources and believing what you hear. Your therapist won't try to talk you out of the political conspiracy theory you think is true. If you're generally healthy, both mentally and physically, it isn't anyone's job to also help you be "right" about your perceptions of reality. You were on your own for that until you wisely started reading this book.

I'll be like a rogue magician who breaks the Magician's Code and explains to you how the tricks are done. You won't need to be a magician yourself to understand what makes a trick work. The "magic" in a magic show is mysterious only until you hear how it is done. Likewise, when I explain to you the walls of your mental prisons, the walls will first become more visible and then start to dissolve with little or no effort on your part.

Once you learn to see the walls of your mental prison, and you learn how to escape, you will have better tools to help usher in what I call the Golden Age. I'll talk more about that in a later chapter.

This is an incredible time in human history. Most of our problems with resource shortages are solved, or solvable, so long as we get our mental game in order. I'll help you do just that.

CHAPTER 2

Political Warming

I wrote this book to help you navigate a world in which the guardians of reality have abandoned their posts. If you live in the modern world, there's a 99 percent chance you are living in a bubble-reality just like your neighbors. And you might be confused about why people who are in different bubbles can't see the wisdom and truth in everything you say. Your bubble doesn't have a communication channel to the other bubbles. When you try to convince others that your worldview is true, the other bubbles put up their shields and don't let your point of view in. They have their own realities and there is little you can do to change that from the outside unless you are a trained and experienced persuader.

Complicating matters, other people will accuse you of being the one in the bubble. And on that point at least, they are probably at least half right. Generally speaking, you can recognize when others are in bubble realities created by their own loserthinking more easily than you can recognize it in yourself.

Our old understanding of reality is rapidly dissolving. Fake news and conspiracy theories have become the building blocks of what we mistakenly believe to be the world we live in. Any two of us can look at the same evidence and have entirely different interpretations of what it all means. Politicians, businesses, and even scientists routinely mislead us. Not always, and not necessarily intentionally, but often enough that we generally can't be sure what is true and what is not.

Recently I saw a debate on television about the cost of single-payer health insurance in the United States. One side said it would cost $32 trillion over ten years. The other side said it would actually save money. That's at least a $32 trillion difference in how the two sides are seeing reality. For reference, $32 trillion is approximately three times the GDP of China. You can't get much further apart than that in terms of agreeing on reality.

The best way to get the sort of attention that drives viewership and profits today is with provocative fake news, which in my way of thinking includes not only factual inaccuracies but also biased coverage and emotion-based presentations. Bias usually reveals itself with something I call opinion stacking. That involves news programming that involves panels of pundits who hold the same biased opinions, joined by only one relatively unpersuasive pundit for the other side.

The technological change that broke the news business was our ability to measure audience reaction to every headline and every variation of every story. Once you can reliably measure the income potential of different approaches to the news, the people who manage the news have to do what works best for profitability or else they are abandoning their responsibilities to shareholders. On top of that, executive compensation is determined by profit performance. From the moment technology allowed us to know which kinds of content influenced viewership the most, the old business model of the news industry was dead media walking. From that point through today, the business model of the press changed from presenting information to manipulating brains.

I want to stress that no one in this story is evil. Everyone is acting according to the well-accepted rules of capitalism, trying to maximize the outcomes for shareholders and their own careers. The main thing that changed was our ability to measure what kinds of content worked best. And when you can measure what works, and you are managing a public business, you are highly incentivized to follow profits, so long as doing so is legal, and in this case it is. Ethics is a separate and important issue, but it isn't predictive in the context of capitalism. If something is legal and profitable, it will happen, a lot.

The inevitable outcome of the press having a business model that rewards brain manipulation versus accuracy is what I call *political warming*. As the press becomes increasingly skilled at stimulating the emotion centers in our brains, one should expect the public to be in a continuous state of fight-or-flight anxiety. We're more scared and angry than I imagine we ever have been, at least since World War II. And that means bigger storms ahead in the form of protests and divisiveness.

As I write this book, the news is full of appeals for more civility in politics. Nearly everyone recognizes that the country is becoming more divided and we are turning on each other in a way we have never seen before. The loserthink way of looking at the situation is that we need to try harder to be nice to each other. But that prescription misdiagnoses the problem. People did not suddenly become different in a fundamental way. The business model of the press manipulated our brains until our emotions overwhelmed whatever traces of rationality we started with. You can't fix that by trying harder to be nice. The influence of the press is too strong, and all because they learned to measure the impact of their actions with extraordinary precision.

In such a world, where truth routinely loses to emotion-based, click-bait versions of reality, how can you know what is true and what is not? And more importantly, how can you act for the greater good—or even your own good—when you can't reliably sort the truth from the lies?

If you buy into the full-scary narratives promoted by either the political left or the political right, you're probably experiencing loserthink. A more useful way to think of the political news is that nearly every major story is exaggerated to the point of falsehood, with the intention of scaring the public. If you think the frightened feeling you are getting from the news is legitimate and appropriate, you probably don't understand how the business model of the news has changed. Twenty years ago, if the media said something dangerous and scary was heading our way, you had to treat that seriously. Today, the news provides one fright after another, but an understanding of why they do it helps you avoid loserthink.

All the doom-and-gloom in the press, and on social media, could give you the impression the world is in big trouble. The reality is almost directly the opposite: things have never been better for humanity, and the future looks incredible too. I'll say more about that in a later chapter.

As you read this book, you are likely to see thoughts with which you agree, and other thoughts you will be certain are wrongheaded. Now that you are warned, I recommend keeping in mind the most important thing you will ever understand about the human experience: *Being absolutely right and being spectacularly wrong feel exactly the same.* That's the right frame of mind for this book.

Let's look at some practical examples in which people who are experienced in different disciplines have advantages in thinking about their world, and therefore also navigating it successfully.

CHAPTER 3

Thinking Like a Psychologist

If you have a background in psychology, you are probably better equipped than the average person in seeing past the common illusions that influence our perceptions. For the purposes of this book, I'll focus on the illusions that I see most commonly displayed on social media and in the news.

THE MIND READING ILLUSION

If your complaint about other people involves your belief that you can deduce their inner thoughts, you might be in a mental prison. We humans think we are good judges of what others are thinking. We are not. In fact, we are dreadful at it. But people being people, we generally believe we are good at it while also believing other people are not.

I've been a public figure for decades, and I've been the subject of intense public criticism—for one thing or another—for most of that time. I'm not complaining, because criticism comes with the job, and I knew what I was getting into. The interesting thing is that perhaps 90 percent of the criticism I receive involves strangers incorrectly

24

assuming what I must be thinking. A quick check of my Twitter feed shows . . .

—Someone claiming I am an advocate for lying

—Someone claiming I approve of neo-Nazis

—Someone claiming I am lying about a fact in order to "sell a book"

—Someone claiming I will defend the president's actions no matter what those actions are

That's just a typical morning for me. None of those claims are true, by the way. And all of them depend on strangers believing they can look beyond my actual words to divine my secret thoughts. That gives me an unusually clear window into how often humans act as if they can read minds. If you someday become famous, you'll see what I'm talking about. Your critics will also misunderstand your inner thoughts while being sure they are doing no such thing.

Even the people who know me best can't accurately deduce what I am thinking more often than chance would suggest. Apparently I look and act exactly the same when I'm either angry or concentrating on writing a funny tweet. And there's not much difference between my bored look and my hungry look. Your experience might be similar.

The impact of all this faulty mind reading is that you and I are often penalized for what other people think we are thinking. I don't want to be punished for other people's faulty thoughts. I'll bet you don't want to be punished for other people's thoughts either.

If your opinion depends on knowing the inner thoughts of a stranger, or even someone close to you, then you might be in a mental prison. You can only know what people say and do, and even that knowledge is likely to be incomplete or out of context. And you definitely can't tell what others are thinking as often as you believe you can. It just feels as if you have that ability. It is an illusion.

If you spend any time on social media, or you follow the news, you know an alarming percentage of political differences are based on mind reading. It looks like this:

PERSON 1: I want healthcare insurance for all citizens.

PERSON 2: Your real goal is total socialism.

PERSON 1: No, I like capitalism, but with social safety nets in some areas.

PERSON 2: Nice try, Karl Marx. I know what you *really* want. You're not fooling anyone!

The mind reading isn't limited to one side of the political spectrum. Here's another example.

PERSON 1: I favor merit-based immigration policies.

PERSON 2: In other words, you want fewer brown people, you racist.

PERSON 1: No, I want people from all over the world who will be good citizens and contribute. Most of them will be nonwhite because the world is mostly nonwhite.

PERSON 2: Nice try, Hitler.

To be fair, no one in these examples believes they are doing mind reading. They think their interpretation of events is so obvious that any simpleton could see what they see.

As I write this chapter, critics are accusing politician Ron DeSantis of racism for calling his Florida gubernatorial opponent, an African-American man, "articulate." On top of that, DeSantis also said on a different occasion that he didn't want anything to "monkey this up," a reference to the political gains he claimed had already been made. Critics say DeSantis was sending a "secret racist dog whistle" to his base. The assumption his critics make is that because they understand the words *articulate* and *monkey* to be racially offensive in the context that each was used, DeSantis must have known it too. And if he knew he was using offensive racial terms, he must be doing it intentionally to signal to racists. Therefore, he must be a racist.

A quick check on Twitter confirms that plenty of educated people were unaware that *articulate* has historically been considered an offensive backhanded compliment when directed at a black man or woman. Was DeSantis one of the people who knew that word was offensive in the context he used it, or was he one of the many people who did not know it? We can't read his mind, so we don't know. We can know what he says and what he does, but we can't reliably know what he is thinking.

People who know the word *articulate* is offensive to African-Americans probably assumed DeSantis knew it too. People who had never heard of that word being an insult to African-Americans probably assumed DeSantis didn't know it either. In effect, both groups acted as if they could read DeSantis's inner thoughts based on the assumption DeSantis's mind is similar to theirs.

The same point applies to DeSantis's "monkey it up" gaffe. Reasonable observers know that any monkey reference would be offensive in the context of discussing a black candidate. But other people who are just as reasonable see it as nothing but an interesting choice of words, probably conflating the more common terms *monkey around* and *mess it up* into "monkey it up." And because both sides of the political divide believe DeSantis thinks the same way they do, the two sides came to inhabit separate realities constructed from their illusions that they can read the mind of a stranger.

If we are being objective about DeSantis, all we can say for sure is that he made two political/verbal mistakes that many people would have known to avoid, while many other people would not have known to avoid them. We can observe that using those words caused DeSantis unnecessary political problems, but we can't know his inner thoughts. If you are certain you know the inner thoughts of a stranger, that's a sign you might have too much confidence in your opinion.

My take on the DeSantis situation is that it is hard to imagine a person who is smart enough to be a major-party candidate for governor (and since this writing has become governor) but also so dumb that he thinks acting like a gigantic racist before the election would work in his favor in the modern world. I can't imagine any reality in which one person can be that smart and that dumb at the same time, at least on a conscious level. In my view, the best explanation for DeSantis's mistakes is that he didn't know his words were offensive.[1]

How likely is that?

Politicians are routinely ignorant on particular topics. Ask your senator what a gallon of milk costs. And if your senator knows the answer, please tell me, because I have no idea what milk costs. Educated and well-informed people always have huge gaps in their knowledge of the world.

Some people might argue that DeSantis's choice of words reveals his subconscious bias, and that's bad enough. But that is not a standard you would want society to adopt. Imagine a coworker reporting you to human resources because he believes your use of ordinary words identifies you as a bigot. That isn't a world you would enjoy. Your coworkers are not good at deducing your private thoughts from the breadcrumbs of your vocabulary.

Verbal gaffes are fairly normal for people running for office. My bias is to prefer ordinary explanations for our observations as opposed to extraordinary ones, assuming the facts support both views.

For example, the famous Pizzagate conspiracy theory of 2016 claimed that a pizza joint in Washington D.C. was the front for a pedophile ring involving both Bill and Hillary Clinton.[2] If that had been true, which it wasn't, it would have been quite an extraordinary situation. Compare that to the more ordinary explanation, that people routinely spread ridiculous conspiracy theories on social media. On day one of the Pizzagate news, I chose the ordinary explanation—that it was fake. A twenty-eight-year-old man chose the extraordinary version and brought an assault weapon to the pizza place to see if he could save those children. He was arrested.

When the news reported in 2017 that a possible "sonic weapon" had been used on diplomatic staff at the U.S. embassy in Cuba, without any obvious motive, I chose the ordinary explanation—that it was a case of mass hysteria. If you are not a student of history and psychology, you might not be aware of how common mass hysteria is. I know how common it is, so I picked the most ordinary explanation of events. At this writing, some experts still believe a sonic weapon was involved, but no confirming evidence has been identified. Keep in mind that we live in an age in which nearly every crime can be solved if we apply enough resources. This one has not been solved, which supports my "ordinary" interpretation that no sonic weapon was involved. I do think some of the folks in the embassy had genuine health problems, but we might never know the causes.[3]

I PREFER ORDINARY explanations to extraordinary ones, but that doesn't always make me right. Sometimes the less ordinary explanation is the correct one. It just doesn't happen often. If you are wondering if you are in a mental prison, it might help to keep these two rules in mind:

> If your opinion depends on reliably knowing another person's inner thoughts, you might be experiencing loserthink.

And . . .

> If an ordinary explanation fits the facts, but you have chosen an extraordinary interpretation instead, you might have too much confidence in your opinion.

I assume most famous people have so often had the experience of strangers incorrectly reading their minds that they regard it as frustratingly normal. If you are not famous, you probably have less appreciation of how often the mind reading illusion is warping people's views of just about everything.

Branding People Evil

If you spend more than five minutes on the Internet, you'll notice people branding other people as apologists, racists, trolls, and other words that mean "evil." That's usually a form of loserthink.

Just to be clear, if you are talking about someone who keeps the remaining parts of his victims in a freezer in his basement, go ahead and call that person evil. I'd call it mental illness, but I don't see much downside in labeling it evil at the same time. In this example, I'm assuming there is no doubt on the facts of the case.

The loserthink comes into play when we imagine we can read people's minds (as opposed to observing their actions) and we totally-definitely see some evil in there. We humans did not evolve to be mind readers. We did evolve to jump to ridiculous conclusions while imagining we did not. So if you are playing the odds, your confidence that you can see some evil in another person's soul is probably closer to being batshit crazy than to being the first known human with psychic powers.

We like to think we can judge people's relative goodness and evilness by observing their actions, but that only works with the easy stuff, such as crime and bullying, and then only when we are sure of the facts. A more typical situation is that people have different ideas of how to reach a greater good in this world. You might think capitalism is the only way to a better world, while someone else thinks we should focus more on fairness and sharing, which you might call socialism. No one in my example has evil intentions, but one of those approaches is likely to be better than the other in achieving something like a greater good. Preferring one plan to another in the quest for a better world is not evil. It is loserthink to act as if it is.

If you think you can gaze into the soul of a stranger and see evil, you might be experiencing a loserthink hallucination.

Socialists and Racists

If you are dismissing your critics with labels they would not assign to themselves, you might be engaged in loserthink. If you call people who want everyone to have good healthcare a bunch of socialists, or you call people who want strong immigration control racists, you are not part of the rational debate. People who have good arguments use them. People who do not have good arguments try to win by labeling.

If your criticism depends on assigning labels instead of cause-and-effect reasoning, you are engaged in loserthink.

OCCAM'S RAZOR

Occam's razor is the idea that the simplest explanation of events is usually the right one. The problem with that line of thinking is that it is complete nonsense, and people who have training in the field of psychology can see the problem right away. In a scientific setting, the simplest explanation that fits the facts is generally preferred. But in the messier nonscientific world, we all think our explanations of the world are the simplest ones.

CREATIONIST: God created everything. Simple!

SCIENTIST: Evolution created everything. Simple!

Occam's razor, as it is typically used in debate, is an example of backward thinking. We think we come to our opinions by looking at the various competing explanations and picking the simplest one that fits the data. Sometimes I suppose that is exactly what happens, especially in uncomplicated situations. But for any complicated or "big" question, it is just as likely, if not more, that we arrive at our opinions by some combination of irrational influences and then defend our position by declaring it to be the simplest explanation.

Occam's razor reminds me of someone trying to throw an anvil at an enemy. If you could lift an anvil and throw it a mile, it would be a powerful weapon. But you can't, so it isn't. Similarly, if people could accurately deduce which of several competing explanations is the simplest one, Occam's razor would mean something. But we can't. So it doesn't.

In science, the simplest explanation that fits the facts is preferred. In life, we are all under the illusion that our explanations of things are the simplest ones.

PROJECTION

In the field of psychology there is a phenomenon called projection. The simple description of projection is that people accuse others of having the flaws the accuser possesses and the target might not. For example, a liar might accuse an honest person of being a liar, and might actually believe it. Or a thief might accuse others of stealing—that sort of thing.

My view on projection is that a professional with a background and education in psychology, who has spent time with a particular client, might be capable of diagnosing projection. And it makes sense that a liar would have a filter on the world in which everyone else is lying too. So I do think projection is a real thing, and I assume professionals can identify it in individuals more often than chance would suggest. The problem occurs when people on social media who are neither mental health professionals nor personally familiar with the target of their comments diagnose strangers as experiencing projection. That's closer to loserthink than science.

I don't believe the average person can tell the difference between an opinion based on observation and something we would properly label projection. If I accuse you of being a liar, it might be because I'm a liar who is projecting, but it could easily be that I'm right and I have caught you in more than one lie. Those situations look the same, and realistically we're

33

usually not in a position to do fact-checking. Humans aren't good fact-checkers. As evidence of that claim, see every discussion of politics ever.

No matter the topic, all sides typically believe they have the right facts and the other side is delusional. No matter which side is right on any given topic, the one thing we know for sure is that being right and being wrong feel exactly the same to all of us. We can't tell the difference. If we could, everyone would agree on everything important.

In the exchange below, Rob Reiner makes some claims about the president's character, and we see a commenter label it as projection. It would be more accurate to say Reiner is engaged in the mind reader form of loserthink in which he apparently believes he can deduce the

inner thoughts of a stranger. We have no expertise to diagnose him as projecting.

> Psychological projection is a real phenomenon, but if you think untrained people can identify it in strangers, you might be experiencing loserthink.

THE EGO PROBLEM

There are two ways to look at the thing we call ego. One of those ways is extraordinarily useful. The other way is loserthink. And by that I mean it almost guarantees you will be unsuccessful in your career and your personal life.

The productive way to think of your ego is to consider it a tool, as opposed to a reflection of who you are on some core level. If you think your ego is a tool, you can choose to dial it up when needed and dial it down when it would be an obstacle.

When we humans hold a higher opinion of our abilities than the facts warrant, that mindset can lead to better results in sports, test taking, romance, our social lives, careers, and more. That's because confidence is strongly correlated with success. The sweet spot for self-confidence involves operating with a belief that you can do more than the available evidence suggests, but not so much more that it would be crazy.

For example, I wouldn't let my ego tell me I could someday play in the NBA. That's crazy. But I might allow my ego to tell me I could become rich enough to own an NBA team. That outcome is highly unlikely too, but not full-tilt crazy, given that I am ambitious by nature and already mildly wealthy. In this example, my confidence that I can beat the odds might help motivate me in that direction in a productive way.

A smaller example involves talking yourself into believing you are the best applicant for a job that many others are trying to get. That belief can come across as confidence, which is a good state of mind to take into a job interview. Confident people perform better under stress. But you don't want to crank up your ego too much because then you would come across as arrogant. Lying to yourself a little bit—to boost your ego—can be productive. But don't overdo it.

Dialing Up Your Ego

When I need to dial up my ego, I remind myself that the people I am about to deal with are a lot like me, in the sense that they too are only pretending to be confident and capable. The world is not a fair place, and there is a good chance the people you are dealing with did not get to where they are because of their intelligence, hard work, and character. As you gain experience in life, that truth becomes more obvious. We're all putting on an act and hoping the audience buys it. Your act might be somewhat close to your true nature, or it might not be. But it is an act nonetheless. Once you embrace the reality that we all present the "enhanced" versions of our real selves, all the time, you can relax a bit and get into character. It is frightening to believe you are the pretender in a room full of confident professionals. Luckily, that is rarely a description of reality. The common situation—and the one you should treat as true—is that we are deeply flawed humans pretending to be otherwise. You aren't the one defective person in the room. Ever.

I find it is also helpful to do self-talk along the lines of "I'm good at this," even if you don't quite believe it on a rational level. This is part of the useful process of faking it until it becomes real. You can literally talk yourself into being more confident by repetition alone.

Breathing and body posture are also huge variables in controlling your confidence in a given situation. Learn how to breathe properly, inhaling through your nose, exhaling through your mouth, and lowering your diaphragm when you inhale, as opposed to shallow breathing in your chest. Practice proper breathing techniques regularly, especially before going into a tense situation.

Your body language will also influence your ego and confidence. Keep your posture straight and your body "open" as opposed to crossing your legs and arms. Take up as much space in the room as you comfortably can, including speaking with your hands. This signals to others that you are confident, but it also has the benefit of triggering you to be more confident because your mind associates open posture with confidence. It's a two-way effect. You can test this on your own by seeing how you feel with crossed arms and a hunched back. Then do the opposite, opening up your arms, straightening your back, and breathing properly. You can feel the difference immediately.

If you are not an extrovert by nature, personal interactions can be awkward, and that can dampen your confidence. The best and easiest defense is to have some questions prepared to fill any gaps. This is especially true for job interviews. Asking smart questions will make you look like a star compared to anyone who simply responds to questions. When you become a good question-asker, you look like the most confident person in the room, and your questions give you a sense of control over the situation, which is good for your confidence.

Learn to make eye contact and to smile. And learn to give a confident handshake. If you do those three things, almost everyone with whom you interact will form a good first impression of you as a confident person. First impressions are sticky. And when people see you as confident, they will treat you as if you are, which reinforces your actual confidence.

Another good trick involves thinking about the things you are good at, to remind yourself of your talents and determination. If you aren't good at anything in particular, try to fix that situation. Find a sport, hobby, or other activity you can practice until you are good at it. Being good at anything makes you more confident in unrelated things. Once you experience being a beginner at something and then improving, you start to see every skill that you don't already have as something you can acquire.

I also recommend regular exercise as a way to drain off your extra energy and keep your nerves in check. Your fitness level will also directly influence your sense of confidence. If you are fit, you will look more attractive, and that will make you feel more confident in any situation.

When you are fit, you will feel more confident in any situation.

For your convenience, I summarize these techniques here.

- Tell yourself, "I'm good at this"
- Learn to breathe properly
- Improve your posture
- Manage your body language
- If you are an introvert, keep some questions in your back pocket so you can guide conversations and always have something to say
- Make a good first impression with a solid handshake and eye contact
- Remind yourself of the skills you are good at
- Exercise regularly to drain off nervous energy

I'm a seasoned media professional, having done many hundreds of interviews. I've given speeches to hundreds of packed venues and navigated all manner of business and social situations. I still practice the methods I described above before I enter any new situation. Managing your ego and your confidence is a lifelong system.

Dialing Down Your Ego

Life will serve up a variety of situations in which you might want to dial down your ego. For example, when you find yourself in a disagreement at work or in your social life, it can be helpful to remind yourself that the other person might be right this time. This is one of the reasons I recommend keeping track of how often you have been certain about something and later learned you were dead wrong. For example, if you believe a political situation will unfold in a certain way, make a specific prediction and write it in a diary, share it on social media, or tell a loved one who is likely to later remind you if you are wrong. The important thing here is to commit to predictions based on your worldview and make a big deal about them so they are harder to forget. Put your predictions into the world outside your head so you have a chance of checking them later without the problem of selective memory.

If you are like most people, you will learn your track record of predicting the future is worse than you imagine. That sort of humility is essential for breaking out of your mental prison. Keep a few examples of your wrongness fresh in your memory so you can generate the right level of humility about your omniscience in future situations.

Don't think of your past mistakes as flaws when you can as easily reframe them as learning experiences, because they are. Once you can embrace the educational value that comes with being wrong, you will find it easier to think, "But I might be wrong this time," in any given situation.

There will be occasions in which you want to dial down your ego to avoid looking like a jerk. For example, sometimes you might need to pretend in front of others that you have some doubts about your opinion, even if you don't. The alternative would be to look like an arrogant know-it-all. Don't hesitate to fake humility when the situation calls for it. But don't overdo it. On the whole, people prefer confident people.

A PERSON WHO considers ego a reflection of self, instead of a tool that one can dial up or down as needed, has fewer pathways to success. Imagine a potential boss asking if you would be willing to start in a position that is below your current job status but has more potential for growth if you perform well. The person who sees ego as who they *are* will reject an offer that feels insulting. The person who sees ego as a tool might take that job and have confidence it will lead to something far better.

I use that example because I once let my ego be my guide in declining a job offer from a top executive at a bank where I once worked. The job offer was to be a "gofer" (an unimportant assistant) to the executive. It would have been a step down, ego-wise, compared to the job I had managing a small workgroup. My coworker who later accepted that job made important contacts in the executive offices and soon became one of the youngest vice presidents the bank ever produced. That would have been my career path had my ego not gotten in my way.

People often ask me how to get into the cartoon business. Usually they show me samples of their comics. About 90 percent of the time my advice is rejected for pure ego reasons. The word *ego* never comes up, but some form of "artistic integrity" is almost always implied, and that's the same thing for our purposes here. People who want to create "art" for a living do not want to hear what the public wants. They want to hear that their ideas are amazing, even when they aren't.

That's ego. And when your ego makes your decisions for you, that's loserthink.

Some years ago, one young cartoonist who had not achieved much commercial success invited me to lunch to pick my brain. I talked with him for two hours, dispensing my best advice on the topic. He took notes, followed up several times for clarifications, and then implemented much of what I suggested. His name is Stephan Pastis. His comic strip, *Pearls Before Swine*, is now one of the top comic strips in the world, and he's a multimillionaire.

You might think Stephan Pastis has no ego because he so seamlessly incorporated my commercial suggestions into his art. That would be far from true. He can dial up his ego like few people you have ever seen. But I observe him doing so when it has some obvious utility, and dialing it down when it would be a problem. For Pastis, ego is a tool. And that mindset plus an impressive talent stack made him rich. I've seen lots of wannabe cartoonists with sufficient talent to succeed. But rarely do you find one who understands how to get out of ego jail.

When my comic strip, *Dilbert*, first appeared in newspapers back in 1989, the topics I addressed were the ones I personally thought were funny. It was mostly generic humor on any topic that caught my attention. But the audience informed me via thousands of email messages that they preferred comics in which Dilbert was at the office. Had I thought of my ego as a reflection of who I am at some core level, as opposed to a tool, my "artistic integrity" probably would have prevented me from taking advice from the audience. But my work experience and education at the time were in the realm of business. In that domain, the customer is the boss, and you do what customers ask whenever it is practical to do so. And that's how I played it. I ignored my own preferences about what was funny and retooled the *Dilbert* comic to be a workplace comic strip. In other words, my ego was a tool, not a prison. And that was the key that unlocked the value I had to offer the world.

In the past few years, I have been building an audience on Periscope, a video streaming app. When I started out, I knew I had what the entertainment industry calls "a face for radio." My voice quality is iffy and I clear my throat and sniff a lot. I'm too old for this sort of thing, and I wasn't qualified to talk about most of the topics I covered. If I had a normal ego, I would have never attempted such a career move. But I wanted to add that skill to my talent stack, and I didn't have a special goal beyond that. My first several months on Periscope were awkward, unfocused, and unpopular. The most common comments were about my ugliness. Young people tried to shame me off the platform by pointing out that it was designed for people younger than a hundred years old.

When you are in an environment that is so casually cruel, people who see ego as a reflection of self are tempted to retreat. But I see ego as a tool, which in this case allowed me to gain experience in a new medium, get a lot of exposure, and build my talent stack. Today, most of the major news media companies follow me on Periscope, and so do a lot of political players at all levels. How important is that? In today's world, influence is determined by a combination of communication skills and reach. I'm a trained hypnotist who writes about persuasion, and now I have a direct communication channel to an enormously important audience. That was possible only because I defied the prison guards of my ego jail who told me I was too ugly and ignorant for Periscope. They weren't entirely wrong, but they were certainly irrelevant, and I treated them as such.

I often observe people who desperately want to win political arguments but can't escape from their own ego jails. People want to be 100 percent right while painting their debate opponent as 100 percent wrong. Sometimes that leads to absurd positions that defy both reason and facts. The need to be right (driven by ego) crowds out the opportunity to be persuasive, which is the whole point of debate. Choosing ego over effectiveness is classic loserthink.

Effectiveness is more important than ego.

Recently I found myself in a loserthink trap in which I imagined my performance was a reflection of self-worth. As a result of that imagined reality, I became irrationally worried about embarrassing myself using a self-service car wash. The nearest full-service car wash involves a long wait and a bit of a drive. So my car was filthy, and I had no solution that was okay with both my schedule and my ego. I didn't want to confess my weird fear of self-service car wash systems to anyone and appear a fool. And I didn't want to give it a try on my own and be the only idiot in the Tri-Valley area who couldn't master the car wash instructions. In my imagined future, I would somehow end up sideways in the car wash, and they would have to dismantle the building to free me. The headlines would read "Idiot Cartoonist Destroys Car Wash."

You might be wondering how I can be smart enough to write books and generally navigate life's complexities and yet be thwarted by a car wash that people of all types seem to master without any special effort. My problem is that I'm too literal to understand directions that are apparently obvious to others. If a sign says *Wait Here* and the cashier waves me up for service, I'm momentarily frozen by the ambiguity of the situation. I might be able to work my way out of that dilemma, but not until I first ask for clarification: "Excuse me. Do you have the authority to override this sign?"

If you think I am underestimating my ability to figure out the car wash system, consider this recent story. My gym, at which I have been a member for about thirty years, recently changed how its lockers work. This upgrade did not go well for me. The old system required members to insert their membership cards inside a slot behind the open door and leave it there in order to remove the key. As you might imagine, lots of members would forget to remove their cards after their workouts, and that was a hassle for the gym and the members. Recently, after having this bad system for decades, they realized there was no reason to require members to put their membership cards in the locker. The gym placed blank cards in all the locker slots so we didn't need to use our membership cards at all. The new system had the same functionality as before, but no risk of people leaving their membership cards in the slots. The gym management even wrote *Do Not Remove* on the blank cards so you knew you didn't need to use your membership card. Good upgrade, right?

Not for this member. I had used the old locker system approximately seven thousand times, I calculated (literally). I stood and stared at that blank card that said *Do Not Remove* and I was stumped. "If I don't remove the card, how will I insert my membership card?" I wondered. So first I tried wedging my card in the same slot with the blank card already in it. It didn't fit. I was so stumped that I left the locker room and asked an employee how the new system works. She explained that all I needed to do was remove the key because the blank card was doing the work my membership card used to do. But she was not succinct, and I lost interest about halfway through her explanation. I gave up on asking for help and returned to see if I could conquer this new system on my own with a little more effort.

In the end—and I don't like to admit this degree of rule breaking—I realized that if no one was looking, I could remove that blank card, insert my member card in its place, and no one would be the wiser. That's what I did. Worked like a charm, but I felt like a criminal all afternoon.

This method continued to work on other visits until I noticed the gym started cutting the blank cards in half so there was not enough showing above its slot to grab and remove it. Then, and only then, did I realize the point of the new system: I didn't need to use my membership card at all. I was so programmed after decades of the old system that I was cognitively blind to the obvious benefits of the improved system. And based on the half-size cards they now use, apparently I was not alone. We gym members had been programmed by years of habit and we were stuck in our mental prisons.

I also have a bad history with the self-checkout stations at my local Safeway grocery store. In my defense, the instructions for those things were obviously written by Russian spies as part of their plan to rip apart the fabric of our society. Based on my history of bad experiences, I have good reason to believe public instructions in any context are a surefire way for me to invite embarrassment and public loathing for being "that guy" who holds up the line. This is clearly an area I needed to work on to reduce my own loserthink.

> If you think ego is who you are, as opposed to a tool you can dial up and down as needed, you might be experiencing loserthink.

Our egos control us through fear, and often that fear is an illusion. Consider public speaking, for example. If you are like most people, you are afraid of making a fool of yourself by talking in public. But that is a false fear. If I asked you to make a list of all the people who looked like fools while doing public speaking, your list would probably be empty. Part of the reason is that most people are not great at public speaking and you wouldn't necessarily notice if someone was extra bad at it.

More importantly, five minutes after you finish listening to a public presentation, you've already forgotten it. Strangers are not that interested in people they don't know. Here are the two key exercises you can use over your lifetime to keep your ego from being your jailer.

Put yourself in potentially embarrassing situations on a regular basis for practice. If you get embarrassed as planned, watch how one year later you are still alive. Maybe you even have a funny story because of it.

And . . .

Note how other people's embarrassments mean little to you when you are an observer. That's how much your embarrassments mean to them: nothing.

Using those two techniques, I have evolved from being embarrassed about just about everything to having almost no sense of shame whatsoever. Like most things in life, practice matters. If you practice controlling your ego, you can learn to do it effectively over time. It doesn't happen overnight, but if you work at it, you'll see big gains in a year. And the gains will accumulate.

FOCUSING ON WHAT IS WRONG

Human nature forces us to focus most of our energy and attention on whatever is going wrong in our world. You wouldn't want to change that human trait because it is a big part of what allows us to survive and improve. When I pick up my mobile phone, I no longer see a modern miracle of technology and human ingenuity. I see a device that keeps interrupting me. Sometimes I wish it had a longer battery life so there would be one less thing to interrupt its job of interrupting me. That sort of flaw-first way of looking at the world is what leads to change. We humans see problems and we automatically wonder how we can fix them. Then we try.

As I write this chapter, I find myself looking past my computer screen, on which everything is going great, as you can plainly see, to notice the tablecloth doesn't reach the edge of the table. That imperfection bothers me even though it is one of the least important variables in my environment. But I can't help obsessing over it, because my brain is a flaw-finder by nature.

On the plus side, my view of the city is terrific, I'm in a great mood, and I'm enjoying some delicious coffee. My experience right now is better than that of 99 percent of humanity. I should be focusing on that.

And I would. But that darned tablecloth.

Give me a minute to fix that.

Okay, I'm back.

Our semi-evolved brains can't handle all the things that are going right in our world because that would involve consciously processing far more information than we can handle. It makes sense that we evolved this way. If your cave-dwelling ancestors were enamored with the beauty of the scenery instead of, let's say, the herd of carnivorous dinosaurs stampeding their way, they would not have survived to create the miracle that is you.

Are you wondering why the author of this book is so dumb he thinks humans and dinosaurs lived at the same time? I'll bet many of you noticed that flaw and it captured your attention for a moment. See what I mean? Flaws are sticky. We can't look away.

The obvious downside of our obsession with life's imperfections is that we can too easily make ourselves crazy. Perhaps that wasn't such a big problem before the age of smartphones and click-bait media. In olden times, the problems that intruded on people's thoughts were hyperlocal. Today, we see problems everywhere in the world. Many of them aren't even real.

As a demonstration, I will pick up my smartphone right now and tell you what problems I see.

My home screen has an emergency warning of dust
    storms approaching. (I'm in Las Vegas at the moment.)
    I didn't even know that was a risk in Las Vegas until
    this minute.
I just learned via text message that my driver's license is
    expired, which matters because I don't know how I'm
    going to get onto a flight home without identification.

My Top Stories app informs me of various political crises,
a deadly disaster in another state, a huge demographic
problem approaching, and a dozen other tales of woe.

That's just a sample. I haven't even opened my email or Twitter, and
you can imagine what horrors they hold for me. Thanks to the miracle of
technology, I can feel angst about every problem in the known universe,
so long as those problems can be described in words or pictures. The
negativity can be overwhelming. I'm sure you've noticed.

On top of our instinct to notice problems, the business model of
the press involves making you think about everything that is going
wrong in the world. It isn't news if someone does a good job and
gets a good outcome. Or at least it isn't the exciting kind of news that
gets clicks.

When you combine a human brain that is wired to notice problems
with a press that is incentivized to present stories involving huge problems, you can easily start imagining that the world is falling apart in a
variety of fatal ways. And that worldview might limit your ability to
appreciate all the things going right.

We live in a world in which lots of things do go wrong. But if all you
see are the flaws in a given situation, you might be cognitively blind to
the bigger picture. You have probably seen people who are locked into a
belief that everything is going wrong and the future looks bleak. In reality, rarely does everything go wrong, and humans are quite handy at
avoiding the worst-case scenarios when they see them developing. Persistent negativity is a harsh mental prison. Humans need optimism and
hope to fuel progress. If all you see is the negative, while those around
you seem to be experiencing optimism, that's a signal you might be in a
mental prison.

If you can't think of anything good about a situation, and yet you observe that others can, you might be experiencing loserthink.

Your best defense against the negativity served up by your own filters on the world is to intentionally seek out positive thoughts and stories, which I sometimes call managing your mental shelf space. For instance, I toggle back and forth between CNN and Fox News to get a more balanced approach to the news, and my trigger to switch is any pharmaceutical commercial I see. This system has the advantage of preventing me from hearing a laundry list of the side effects associated with each drug. If you allow yourself to listen to unnecessary lists of horrible health issues, the experience will depress your mood, create unnecessary stress, wreck your energy and optimism, and probably weaken your immune system. If that seems like an exaggeration, it is not meant to be one. Viewing one commercial isn't much of a danger, but if you watch an hour of cable news, you will hear so many scary references to debilitating health problems in the advertisements that over time it will start to gnaw away at your mind and your body.

It is helpful to think of your mind as having limited shelf space. If you fill that space with negative thoughts, it will set your mental filters to negativity and poor health, and there will be no space left for healthy, productive, and uplifting thoughts. You can control your mental shelf space—to a degree—by manipulating your physical surroundings. In the case of pharmaceutical commercials, it means changing the channel so you are not bombarded with unhealthy thoughts that can wreck your mind and body over time.

I will pause here to note that science is solidly on my side.[4] So is nearly every self-help guru. The thoughts you allow into your head are the code that programs your mind and body. If you watch sad movies, you can become sad. If you hear inspirational stories, you can feel inspired. And your mental state has a huge impact on your health. Exposure to horrible and frightening thoughts can elevate your stress, which releases cortisol. The Mayo Clinic website explains that cortisol "curbs functions that would be nonessential or detrimental in a fight-or-flight situation. It alters immune system responses and suppresses the digestive system, the reproductive system and growth processes. This complex natural alarm system also communicates with regions of your brain that control mood, motivation and fear."[5]

That's what you do to yourself when you expose your mind to unnecessary negativity, such as pharmaceutical commercials, sad movies, sad music, and sad news. It is nearly impossible to avoid all of those sources of negativity, but you can limit their impact by filling your mental shelf space with healthier and more productive thoughts. Every minute you spend with a positive thought is a minute that you keep negative thoughts at bay.

If you are having trouble keeping negative thoughts from your mind, don't try to "not think" about them. That just makes you think about them more. Instead, find the most positive and "sticky" thoughts you can imagine, and focus on them until your mental shelf space is filled.

If you allow your mental shelf space to fill up with negative thoughts, you are punishing yourself with an unhealthy form of loserthink.

Later in this book, I present my case for why we are entering a Golden Age. You might quibble with the details of my optimism, but note how it makes you feel, and let that feeling be your reward as you train yourself to seek good news and positive interpretations of reality. Your natural instinct is to notice problems, but you can train yourself to think more positively and to notice the good in things. All it takes is intention and practice. Try it for a week and you will notice a difference in yourself. You'll probably feel happier and less anxious, but—equally important—you will discover a more accurate filter on reality.

CHAPTER 4

Thinking Like an Artist

FAILURE OF IMAGINATION

A defining characteristic of artists is that they tend to have strong powers of imagination. And that imagination can be helpful in keeping you out of mental prison. But you don't need to have an artist-level imagination in order to see the world more clearly. To keep yourself out of mental jail, continually remind yourself that the most likely explanation for many—if not most—situations in life is *something you didn't imagine.*

Have you ever been angered by someone's apparent selfishness, sloth, lying, incompetence, rudeness, or criminality and later realized

there was a perfectly good reason for whatever they did, and it wasn't for any of those reasons? That situation describes about half of most people's experience of life. We're continually making bad assumptions about why things happened. We humans are a skeptical bunch, and we often think someone or some entity is running a scam on us. Unfortunately, we are often right. But at least half the time, based on my observation, we think a conspiracy exists when there are perfectly normal explanations for events.

I think my dog Snickers believes I'm an idiot because I don't take her outside to play when she is quite clearly communicating to me that it's time to do so. Snickers knows she is sending me the "Let's go outside" signal, she knows I see it, and she knows I am physically able to go outside. So if I don't stop what I am doing and take her out, does she think I'm stupid?

As a rule, we can't always tell the difference between the people who are far smarter than us and the people who are dumber. Both groups make choices we can't understand. That's an important thing to keep in mind. If your opinion is that another person's idea is terrible, you can only be sure that at least one of you is stupid. You can't *really* know which one of you it is except in rare cases in which things can be objectively measured.

I find it useful to remember I can't always tell the difference between genius and stupidity. Neither can anyone else, at least not every time. So when a person who is otherwise smart says something that sounds dumb to me, I remind myself that, in this situation, I might be the dog.

When you have multiple possible explanations for an outcome, such as you might hear from competing sides in a murder trial, you can usually sniff out the truth so long as you have a sincere dedication to facts and reason. Or at least we all hope you can, because otherwise the justice system is nothing but a cruel and expensive placebo. But keep in mind that jury trials are a special situation in which the facts are meticulously explained and a judge helps you decide how to wrestle with those facts. Your normal life is nothing like that. In our daily lives, we're often guessing about the facts based on hints, hunches, bias, misinformation, and the like. It is no wonder so many people are walking around in what looks to you a state of delusional thinking.

The more ordinary way people make bad assumptions is by a failure of imagination. Take, for example, my story about fearing instructions at the self-service car wash. If you had not heard my story, and you saw how dirty my car is, you might think the only explanation that makes sense is that it recently got dirty and I'll be getting it cleaned soon.

You would correctly assume I can afford to get my car washed, and over the course of a month, for example, I would have enough time to get it done. And every semi-normal person prefers a clean car to a dirty one. So when you saw my perpetually dirty car, you might think I didn't wash it because I am too busy, or because I want to preserve water, or because I'm not interested in how my car looks so long as it works. You might come up with a few more reasonable explanations too. The explanation you are unlikely to even imagine is the one that is true: I have an irrational fear of public instructions.

I'll give you two more examples of how a failure of imagination is confused with rational thinking. In the interest of balance, one example comes from the political left and one from the right. Loserthink isn't confined to one group, unfortunately.

The first example comes from an opinion article on CNN's website, in which it asks this question: Why do so many people with racist values embrace the GOP?

I can't read minds, so it is unclear what the author's internal thoughts are. Is he a clever and unscrupulous persuader who knows he

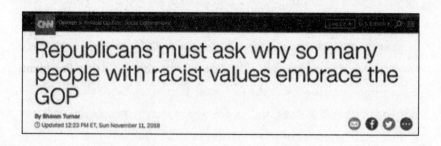

Republicans must ask why so many people with racist values embrace the GOP

By Shawn Turner
Updated 12:23 PM ET, Sun November 11, 2018

is departing from reason and hopes others don't notice? Or is he someone who can't tell the difference between a lack of imagination and a solid argument? We don't need to solve that mystery to see that the argument presented relies on the readers' lacking imagination. I can demonstrate that here by suggesting several perfectly reasonable ways to explain this observation.

One potential explanation is that the writer is suffering from a form of political hysteria that grips both sides of the political divide, albeit at different times and in different ways. The article includes a link to a known hoax—the idea that President Trump called racists in Charlottesville "fine people." That fake news is still widely reported as fact. The president was not referring to the racists, or anyone "marching with them" at Charlottesville, as fine people. He was referring to both sides of the Confederate statue issue as fine people. He clarified his opinion and denounced the racists (as he has done many times) when asked to do so. The existence of a known hoax in the article suggests the writer either believes the hoax, which discredits the rest of his opinions, or he is intentionally promoting a hoax, which also means his opinion lacks credibility. Those are a few explanations I can imagine.

The most ordinary explanation I can imagine for why racists prefer President Trump is that they believe CNN's fake news (using the Charlottesville "fine people" hoax as an example) in exactly the same way nearly every Democrat does. Now add the bias that comes from wanting to believe something, and you have the perfect recipe for confirmation bias.

Another ordinary (and reasonable) explanation is that President Trump's stated goal of treating all Americans the same feels to racists like a better world than whatever they imagine Democrats are offering. I can't read the minds of racists, but one assumes racists believe Democrats will transfer money and influence from white people to people of color, and change the culture at the same time.

It is easy to imagine that racists want fewer brown people to immigrate into the country while mainstream Republicans want tighter border control for economic and security reasons. That would put them on the same side but for entirely different reasons.

I can also imagine that racists have trouble recruiting new members, for obvious reasons, so anytime they can graft their philosophy onto something that is already happening in the world, such as a new president who is strong on border security, it draws attention to their cause in a way they find productive.

If the only explanation you can imagine for why racists back a Republican president is that he is whistling to them in a secret code that nearly every Democrat claims to hear, I suppose anything is possible. But it would border on insane for any politician in the United States to think that strategy is a good one. And it fails to imagine the far more ordinary explanations I just mentioned.

To add some context, I like going to Las Vegas to work on my book and enjoy the food. Other people go to Vegas for the gambling, drinking, and anonymous sex. One of the most normal situations in the world is that people like the same thing (in this case Las Vegas) for wildly different reasons. In politics too, people can support the same candidate for wildly different reasons. To imagine people like a person or a place for the same reasons is a serious lack of imagination and a denial of the most common experience in our shared reality.

A lack of imagination is common to both sides of the political divide. For example, this week I have been bombarded on Twitter by followers of a hoax called Q. Believers in this obvious (to me anyway) hoax say an anonymous person or persons with government insider information is leaking secrets to the public as part of some sort of scheme to support President Trump against so-called Deep State traitors.

The followers of this hoax argue with me that any evidence consistent with Q being a government insider is all you need, so long as you can't imagine any other explanation for what you are observing. For example, President Trump once tweeted a photo that had as its file name "DoitQ," which believers took as a signal that President Trump is pro-Q. Several people asked me on Twitter to explain how that could possibly be the file name unless President Trump was cleverly confirming with this "secret Q whistle" the validity of Q.

I explained on Periscope that the most ordinary explanation is that whoever named the file is a follower of Q. Presidents of the United States rarely get involved in naming files. Maybe it was the work of a prankster or a hacker. And you can't rule out coincidence, given that there is a 100 percent chance the environment would serve up some sort of random Q-related reference that seemed like a cryptic message but isn't. I can't put odds on any of those explanations being the accurate one, and perhaps there are several more explanations I have not imagined. All I can say with a sense of certainty is that it is unlikely a sitting president named a computer file to send a secret message that was disguised as a totally public message.

Q supporters also ask how it could be possible that a prominent Q supporter got a photo opportunity with President Trump in the White House, which happened in the summer of 2018, unless the president was signaling that Q was real. The most ordinary explanation is that the president takes photos with lots of people, and it doesn't mean he knows what they are all up to. In the summer of 2018, I also visited the Oval Office and posed for pictures with the president. It doesn't mean he endorses all of my opinions, or even knows what they are.

Life is messy and unpredictable. Sometimes our underpowered and biased brains correctly deduce a chain of cause and effect. But the accuracy of our opinions is deeply influenced by our ability to imagine alternate explanations for events.

So what do you do about that?

One thing I find helpful is growing old. It's a slow process, but totally worth it compared to dying. Oldsters such as myself have vastly more experience than the young at being simultaneously wrong and also surprised about it. In time, we come to understand how easy it is to be confident in our opinions and yet spectacularly wrong. Or at least we do if we have been keeping score. And that's exactly what I recommend doing. Make a mental note every time you find yourself being wrong about something you thought you couldn't possibly be wrong about. Focusing on your track record can prime you to understand there can be lots of different explanations for a set of facts, and you can't always think of them all.

The failure-of-imagination problem is a risk in every aspect of your ordinary life, from your workplace dramas to your love life. The next time you find yourself generating a belief about why something went wrong, keep in mind that one of the most common explanations for anything in life is *something you didn't imagine.*

If you can't imagine any other explanation for a set of facts, it might be because you are bad at imagining things.

CHAPTER 5

Thinking Like an Historian

O ne of the strongest walls in our mental prisons is a thing called history. And history isn't even real. I mean that in two ways.

The first way history is not real is that whoever is in charge gets to write history any way they like. And the way they like it is whatever way keeps them in power and looking awesome. That means you should expect the history in one country to be substantially different from the history in another, even when discussing the same events. Which history is the accurate one? Answer: neither. Both are filtered through politics and distorted to the point of being misleading if not outright untrue, except for the basic facts such as names and dates.

When I was a kid, I learned in history classes that bold European explorers discovered and settled America. They were well-intentioned folks who tried and largely failed to befriend the Native American population. Unfortunately, said my textbooks, the Native Americans were too primitive to understand important concepts such as private property, and one thing led to another until the European settlers graciously granted Native Americans their own reservations. For free! Somewhere along the line, the Native Americans taught the pioneers how to grow corn. That's the condensed, racist version of history I learned.

But I assume that had Native Americans written our history books, the accounts might look quite different. Those books might say Columbus was a psychopathic monster, and that European invaders pursued genocide to steal land from the locals. Or something along those lines.

As a young person, I took it for granted that my country had the accurate version of history and everyone else was lying or misinformed. It never occurred to me that every government invents its own version of history to brainwash their population. We are raised to assume we are the lucky ones who learn accurate history while evil leaders elsewhere are duping their citizens. I hope you can see how unlikely it is that any country is presenting history to its children in an objective way.[1]

I'm sure history books get most of the big stuff right. For example, slavery really existed, and World Wars I and II really happened. But context matters, and every story can be told multiple ways. Ever since the presidential election of 2016, we have been bombarded with fake news from every political direction. Both sides generate fake news, and lots of it. Which versions will historians choose to put in textbooks? They have multiple realities from which to choose. My bet is that historians will choose versions of history that are best suited for indoctrinating kids to be obedient and productive citizens. Truth will be a secondary consideration, as always, when it comes to socializing children into productive adults.

If you believe you learned an accurate version of history in school, you are probably wrong.

There is a second and more profound way in which history keeps us in mental prison: it can have too strong a hold on us. If you can learn to release that hold, another wall of your mental prison will fall.

In my case, my childhood was horrific in ways I don't like to discuss, and those memories intruded mightily on my adult happiness long after the events themselves dissolved into the nothingness of history. The past didn't exist anywhere except in my memories, but that was enough to ruin my present happiness. I learned that I could control those destructive thoughts by crowding them out with work, intellectual pursuits, and other distractions. Over time, the memories faded from lack of attention, and now I don't consider them to have any impact on my current happiness.

> If bad memories are keeping you from being happy, try crowding out the destructive memories with new and interesting thoughts. Stay busy, in mind and body, and time is on your side.

The best example of history as a mental prison is the Middle East. Almost everyone in that region is anchored to history in one negative way or another. Here is a summary of every debate in the Middle East.

PERSON 1: Do you remember the time people like you did terrible things to people like me?

PERSON 2: That was only because people like you did bad things to people like me first.

PERSON 1: People like you started it!

And so on to infinity.

If you could erase the knowledge of history from every citizen in the Middle East, I suspect it would be easier to live in peace. The trouble happens when people try to manage events in the present to fix the past. That isn't possible. You can't fix the past, and trying to do so generally won't lead to anything good.

From a persuasion perspective, history can be a useful tool. If I can make you feel guilty for something your demographic group did to mine, I might be able to influence you in a way that is good for me. But don't make the mistake of believing that history matters in situations in which all it does is limit how you think about your options. History doesn't have to control you.

History (even the fake kind) can be useful for persuading others through guilt. But don't make the mistake of persuading yourself that history should matter to your choices today.

My life, which has always been strange, got stranger in April 2018 when Kanye West tweeted nine separate outtakes from an online video I made on the Periscope app. I was talking about Kanye's ideas on escaping from "mental prisons."

By then I had become well known for writing about President Trump's persuasion skills. Kanye was famous for lots of things, but somewhere in the top twenty was his public service commercial after Hurricane Katrina in 2005 in which he said, "President Bush doesn't care about black people." So we know Kanye isn't a Republican booster, and that matters to this story.

In 2018, Kanye visited President Trump at the White House and declared that he loved the man, but not necessarily his politics. That unexpected bromance created a dangling thread in the fabric of reality, which Kanye later yanked by retweeting my videos.

It seems that no mental prison can hold Kanye. His "occupation"—if you can call it that—includes rapper, singer, songwriter, music producer, fashion designer, entrepreneur, and political/social activist, to name a few accomplishments. Time magazine named him one of the 100 Most Influential People in the World in both 2005 and 2015. And Kanye has repeatedly teased a run for the presidency in 2024, which I take seriously.

By the time you think Kanye can't or shouldn't do something, he's already doing it. Or in the case of tweeting my videos, doing it nine times. I don't have to tell you that tweeting content from the creator of Dilbert doesn't help you in either your fashion business or your music business. It was a risky move for his brand, and probably no one on earth, including me, would have advised him to do it. He did it anyway. Evidently, he isn't trapped in the mental prison that others would build for him.

Kanye's message was that focusing on the past creates a sort of mental prison that limits your options. In the simplest form, if a white male in America has ten ways to succeed and an African-American only has eight, it isn't productive to focus on the difference. It is more productive to pick a path to success and take it. In the long run, nothing persuades like success. We all have the option of living in a mental prison of the past or creating the future we want. Kanye is a creator.

To put this in context, when problems are huge, you need big tools to fix them. Slavery was a huge problem, and it took a big tool—the Civil War—to fix it. But that wasn't enough to fix racism in America, obviously. The civil rights movement was the next tool, and it was a smaller tool than a civil war, but still enormous in scope and impact. In recent decades, the legal system tried to mop up what it could of remaining racism. That was a smaller tool than the civil rights movement, but still a big tool. Today's "institutional racism" is still a huge problem, say many smart people, but we probably can't fix it with civil wars, civil rights legislation, or lawyers. We need a tool that better fits the task. Kanye suggested moving away from focusing on the past and getting on with the business of succeeding. That makes sense in my worldview, because, as I said, nothing changes minds and creates new options as effectively as success.

President Obama's political genius was that he ran for president on his talent and policies. He didn't ask us to elect an African-American president to compensate for slavery, racism, or anything else. If you want to persuade white people, Obama showed you the gold standard for doing it.

Asian-Americans followed a similar strategy. They too were the victims of intense racism throughout the history of this country. But they also had clear paths to success, and took them. Today, Asian-Americans are doing better in terms of education and economics than most folks in America.

I contend that escaping from our mental prisons is how we will unlock the Golden Age. And to do that, we are best served by focusing on systems for success, as opposed to past injustices. We should not forget or minimize the past, as it serves us in a number of ways. But we can choose to focus on the paths forward instead of the footprints behind us, and as a strategy for success, that mindset is probably the right tool for the job.

Focusing on the past when the present offers sufficient paths to success is loserthink. It is better to focus on your own systems for success, and when you succeed, watch how winning fixes most problems.

DOES HISTORY REPEAT?

If an advanced species from another planet sent a scout to spy on earth and report back, the scout might describe humans this way:

ALIEN SCOUT: "The planet is dominated by some sort of organic robots. Their operating system uses a faulty pattern recognition algorithm that is designed to make it easier for them to hate each other."

Nailed it!

Our tiny brains don't have the capacity to grasp the complexities of life and then process that knowledge to make smart decisions. We only think we can. What we do instead of rational decision-making is employ a sloppy form of pattern recognition to make sense of our world.

There are three important things to know about human beings in order to understand why we do the things we do.

1. Humans use pattern recognition to understand their world.

2. Humans are very bad at pattern recognition.

3. And they don't know it.

We can't tell the difference between valid patterns that might predict something useful and something that simply reminds us of something else but means nothing.

Our meager talents at pattern recognition wouldn't be much of a problem if we realized how often we see meaning in patterns where none exist. When you expect to be fooled, you can be on the lookout for it. But if you expect the opposite—that you will be wise, correct, and sexy in most situations—you are primed to be fooled.

Making matters worse, historians and philosophers have passed down to us some sticky sayings about patterns that we are raised to believe are wise. The worst offender is this one:

"HISTORY REPEATS"

American philosopher George Santayana allegedly said some version of "Those who cannot remember the past are condemned to repeat it." That often gets shortened to "History repeats."

I suppose the idea of history repeating would be useful for someone such as a scholar to add context to history. But one thing you've probably noticed about most of the people with whom you interact is that they are not, in all likelihood, scholars.

I would trust a scholar to know that "history repeats" has no more predictive power than observing that people were selfish, brutal, and violent in the past, so you can reasonably expect more of that in the future. The assumption that people haven't changed much since the start of recorded history feels accurate and useful. But once you extend that observation about people to an observation about a situation, you're on shaky ground.

Let me give you an example. When my first book, The Dilbert Principle, became a number-one bestseller, my publisher asked for a second one to capitalize on the momentum. If "history repeats," how should I have expected my second book to perform? Just as well as the first?

Lots of authors have had bestselling books and then followed up with a second book. You might expect my experience to be similar to that of other authors in my situation. You can probably think of authors who had a huge bestseller and then rode that popularity to create a string of even larger bestsellers. Stephen King, J. K. Rowling, James Patterson, and John Grisham come to mind.

My first bestseller got me scads of attention and lots of happy readers who gave me stellar reviews. I assumed they were spring-loaded to buy my next book too, and I assumed new readers would discover me as well. In other words, I was hoping history would repeat.

I published my follow-up book, *Dogbert's Top Secret Management Handbook*, and it did well enough to top the nonfiction bestseller list. But overall, it sold about half as many books as the first.

Why the heck did history decide to stop repeating just when I needed it???

One day my publisher explained to me that nonfiction books tend to follow the same pattern that mine had. The authors who consistently wrote one bestseller after another were fiction authors. Consumers of fiction want more of the kind of writing they like, only next time with different characters and stories.

Consumers of nonfiction books apparently think some version of "I already know what that author has to say." Especially when the topic seems to be in the same domain as the previous book. The defense against that pattern, for nonfiction writers, is to write books on entirely new topics if the audience lets you get away with it, the way Malcolm Gladwell and Michael Lewis do. I use the same strategy now.

One would need to have a lot of publishing experience to know which historical patterns would be the predictive ones in my situation.

I thought I knew all I needed to know about how one bestseller leads to more. But I didn't. We humans are not good at knowing which history is the one that will repeat. Life is messy and complicated, and the situations we encounter often remind us of multiple histories. But which of those histories is the one that is predictive?

Consider a person who has been married and divorced twice. If that person gets married again, does history suggest a divorce is likely? Or does history suggest that third marriages are more likely to last than first or second marriages? On top of that, what makes this particular couple typical enough to compare to the average? For example, if one of them is a sex addict, isn't that a more predictive variable than the third-marriage pattern? Beats me. The point is that we generally have more than one historical pattern in play. And we usually don't know which ones will be the most predictive.

Consider the stock market. That is a bundle of competing histories. You might be looking at the track records of top management. You might be looking at the history of price competition in this market. You might be looking at the history of unexpected innovations. Every company is a collection of patterns. Which ones matter?

The smartest people in the investment world will tell you the quality of management is the most predictive variable. They will also advise you to buy index funds instead of individual stocks because no one can consistently predict how managers will perform. Maybe the managers of some public companies got lucky with success a few times in the past. Maybe their skills were perfectly suited for the last situation but not this one.

Think of the trillions of dollars swirling around investment markets across the globe. With so much on the line, you can expect to attract the smartest, most capable people in the world. And indeed, top investment advisors come from the best schools and have deep experience. If "history repeats" was a meaningful concept, those experts could easily pick the companies that will perform the best.

They can't.

As I just mentioned, unmanaged index funds almost always beat the individual stock-pickers. As it turns out, the history of broad index funds performing well *does* repeat. Or at least it has so far. By the time you read this book, someone might invent an algorithm that predicts the fate of individual companies in a statistically valid way. Because history repeats until it doesn't. And you never know when the "doesn't" phase starts.

History also has the quality of influencing the future to be different. And by that I mean we learn from mistakes. For example, the United States tried to negotiate with North Korea several times over the decades and found the North Koreans would make promises and later break them. Did that history help predict what would happen when President Trump met with Kim Jong-un? That's like the third-marriage pattern. People learn (eventually) what didn't work last time and so they modify their approach. And if the new approach fails too, they try something else next time. Technologists and marketers call this A/B testing, in which you are heading steadily toward a good outcome while appearing to observers as if you are failing most of the way, at least until something works. A pattern of consistent failure looks a lot like A/B testing that isn't yet complete. One is bad news and the other is good news about to happen. They look the same.

Mark Twain once observed that people can't tell the difference between good news and bad news. That feels right to me. We usually can't tell which patterns are most predictive, which means we literally don't know if we are looking at good news or bad coming our way. But we imagine we can.

By now you might be thinking I have overreached in my criticism of the idea that history repeats. Perhaps you can think of situations in which you are absolutely sure history did repeat. But I submit to you that history is very busy, and it does a lot of stuff. You wouldn't notice all the occasions in which history *doesn't* repeat. In fact, if you were sure you noticed history repeating a thousand times, it wouldn't tell you anything unless you knew how many times it did *not* repeat when it might have. If that number is a million, your observation of a thousand history-repeating situations is no indication that history repeats. In that scenario, it would be more accurate to say sometimes events remind you of history and sometimes they don't. It would not be rational to say there is some sort of predictive relationship between unrelated historical anecdotes and whatever you are doing today.

And when you do see history apparently repeating, ask yourself if you needed to know history to make your prediction. For example, if every time someone challenges a professional MMA fighter to a bar fight, the trained fighter either wins or refuses to fight, that might seem to us like a predictive history. But you could predict the same two probable outcomes with no knowledge of history. The better fighter should be expected to win a fight. And a professional fighter would know that the legal system would treat him harshly for fighting a drunk with no special fighting skills.

Whenever humans have an opportunity to do something illegal that would have a huge payoff should it work, and no risk of getting caught, the odds of someone doing that illegal thing approach 100 percent. Not everyone will take the bait, but if enough people are in that situation, you can be sure at least one will take a run at the free money with no risk, even if it means breaking a law. You might say that's a case of history repeating, because whenever that situation occurs, sooner or later someone will try to take advantage. But here again we need no special knowledge of history to make our predictions. You simply have to understand the dark side of human nature.

For the nitpickers reading this chapter, I acknowledge that we only understand human nature because we observe how people have acted throughout history. History gives us useful insight on how humans act. But that insight is useful only in simple cases.

Will people who are hungry seek food? Yes.

Will people exploit loopholes for personal gain? Yes.

Will people lie if they think it helps a lot and they can get
away with it? Yes.

When we talk about the idea of history repeating, we're usually not talking about the simple and predictable impulses of human beings. Usually we're comparing, for example, one complicated set of negotiations with hundreds of moving parts to some past situation in which the variables were substantially different but we are still reminded of it.

As I was writing this chapter, I took a break and checked Twitter. I happened upon a debate on the value of so-called trickle-down economics, which refers to cutting taxes and hoping that doing so gooses the economy enough to make up the difference in how much the government collects in taxes. The debate went like this:

CRITIC OF TRICKLE-DOWN ECONOMICS: It has never worked in the past.

PROPONENT OF TRICKLE-DOWN ECONOMICS: It has totally worked in the past.

If history repeats, which history will be doing the repeating? I take it as a given that one of those views is right. But how would the average citizen know which was true?

History doesn't repeat, at least not in any way you can use to accurately predict the future. (The exceptions are simple situations.)

THE SLIPPERY SLOPE

The slippery slope argument bothers me more than most forms of loserthink. It is generally presented as an argument that things will continue going in the same direction until they go too far and some form of harm is done.

For example, gun rights folks will argue that any form of gun control is a slippery slope to full confiscation. Some support that argument with appeals to "history repeats" based on the experiences of countries that are quite different from the United States.

My objection to the slippery slope argument is that *everything is a slippery slope until it isn't*. In physics, a body in motion will stay in motion until it meets an equal and opposing force. Our experience of life is a lot like that. Literally everything would be a slippery slope if not for counterforces. So look for counterforces to predict how far a thing will slide. If there are no offsetting forces, then yes, things will keep going in one direction forever. But that's rare. Usually a counterforce pops up as a reaction, or it is already in place.

In the case of gun control in the United States, the counterforce is the gun owners themselves and their commitment to the Second Amendment. They generally favor commonsense rules about gun safety, but if you start knocking on doors to take away guns, that is unlikely to end well. The slippery slope simply doesn't apply. Gun owners might end up with more restrictive rules of ownership than they prefer, but so long as most of the public prefers the new rules, you can't blame the slippery slope. That's just voters getting what they want.

There's also no objective way to know when a slippery slope is more progress than problem. It depends which side you are on. Your slippery slope might be my progress. I like progress, and I don't want you to stop my progress by labeling it a slippery slope.

The slippery slope isn't a concept worthy of using for persuasion, or for any other purpose. It isn't predictive because there is generally a counterforce ahead. And if the counterforce is not evident, or it seems too weak, there's a good chance a stronger counterforce will material-ize specifically to stop the slippery slope.

Belief in slippery slopes is loserthink. It is more useful to look at forces and counterforces to see where things are likely to end up.

PRIVACY IS OVERRATED

Humans probably don't have a biological need for much privacy. We are tribal creatures, meaning we evolved in environments in which the tribe knows everything about you, whether you like it or not. Privacy seems to be more of a modern invention. Most of us appreciate having privacy in a variety of situations. But it's not likely that our preference for privacy is compatible with our nature. Consider that humans also enjoy drugs, cigarettes, and alcohol. Just because we prefer something, that doesn't make it good for us. Privacy has real-world benefits, and I don't recommend you give it up without a fight. But if your desire for some specific forms of privacy is fear based, you might be creating a mental prison for yourself that you don't want.

I think most people would agree that the pivotal step in the advancement of gay rights involved brave activists "coming out" about their sexual orientation and making it safe, in time, for others to do so. You could say the LGBTQ community traded privacy for equality. They didn't give up all of their privacy—only the part that kept them in a social prison. That's the clearest historical example of privacy being more of a problem than a solution. Once the LGBTQ community embraced that truth—that privacy was their prison, not their protection— they had a path out. It wasn't easy, and it might never be easy. But it's a winning path.

Let me tell you about a time in which I intentionally traded privacy for freedom. I was born with a condition called paruresis, also known as shy bladder. It means you can't urinate if anyone else is in the room or even in listening distance. Perhaps 5 percent of the public has this condition. The thing you need to know about paruresis is that there is no way for someone who has it to simply "relax harder" to get past it. The sensation is that your body and your mind become temporarily disconnected. Your body "locks up" even when your mind is totally at ease. The name *shy bladder* is misleading because shyness is not the problem. It happens to people who are not shy in general. And it seems to have a genetic component. At around age fifty, my brother Dave "came out" about his paruresis. At the time, I didn't even know it had a name. And as hard as this is to imagine, I didn't know my brother had it. Nor did he know I had it.

For half a century, my biggest problem in life was one that I believed was unique to me. I kept it private because I didn't want to be seen as a freak. And I didn't want to be judged or mocked for it. My knee-jerk preference for privacy made everything worse. It added the fear of detection to the base problem. And the base problem was bad. Imagine traveling and not being able to use a public restroom except in rare instances when they are empty. Oh, and just to make things interesting, I also have a small bladder. It was a continuous nightmare for fifty years. School was a nightmare. My corporate jobs were a nightmare. Dating was difficult. I was becoming rich and successful with the Dilbert comic and at the same time, to be frank, my quality of life was poor.

About 5 percent of the people reading this book are having an "Oh, shit" moment because I'm talking about them. They are in hiding about their shy bladders too. And their lives are nightmares for the same reasons. I'm about to release that group from their mental prisons.

When my brother started sharing his condition—and we soon found out my late father had it too—everything changed about the way I felt about it. I was no longer the lone freak. I was just one of the people with this condition, which I now had a name for. If you add up the ages of my father, my brother, and me, we went a collective 180 years without knowing anyone else on the planet was suffering from this life-destroying condition, and that added greatly to the psychological weight of it. You might say that pain and fear were our penalty for maintaining our privacy, but none of us knew it at the time.

My brother became an activist in the shy bladder cause. He has a website at paruretic.org, where he teaches fellow travelers how to work through their condition. Step one is admitting your situation to anyone who matters. That takes the pressure off and allows you to say and do what you need to say and do. For example, if I'm with a group of friends and excuse myself to use a public restroom, and one of the guys gets up to do the same, I loudly proclaim that the situation won't work for me because I can't use restrooms when others are in there. Not once has that been a problem or an embarrassment. Turns out most people either have the same problem, or some milder version of it, or know someone who does. More importantly, no one much cares about your problems, at least not your minor health issues, as they see it. We imagine people care about our situations more than they do.

The second part of the solution involves learning to wait at the urinal or in a restroom stall as long as it takes. You might need to wait for several people to come and go. Or you might use a stall with more privacy, if that works for you. You might even use the stall for people with disabilities, with good cause. Over time, you can learn to do what you need to do with no sense of embarrassment. But it takes practice.

Practice is the third part of the process. You practice by choosing increasingly difficult "challenges" that will train your mind and body to cooperate over time. For example, you might practice using a restroom when someone is in the next room. Eventually you can try using a urinal on one end of the restroom when another person is near the other end. At this point in my journey, I can use most public restrooms unless there is a person directly next to me at the urinal, the privacy barrier is low, or the other person got there at the same time. And when that happens, I just wait or use a stall. The net result of relinquishing my privacy on this specific topic is that it reduced the biggest problem in my life to an occasional annoyance. Better yet, for 5 percent of the people reading this book, I just put you on the path to your own recovery.

If you're a weirdo in any way (and I say this with love), you can probably find similar weirdos if you stop hiding. And life will be better for all of you, assuming your weirdness is legal.

I'm not antiprivacy. I take it as a given that there are some situations in which society is better off with a degree of privacy. My point here is that we have a reflexive desire for privacy that is not too far in type from our reflexive desire to eat junk food. The fact that we want privacy is not related to how good it is for us. My examples with LGBTQ and shy bladder "coming out" make the case.

Now consider what it would mean to healthcare outcomes if our lifestyle choices, our health records, our DNA, and even our current health indicators were routinely collected and stored. In this imaginary scenario, let's say the information was private from your neighbors, but available in raw data form without your identification to scientists. Armed with that kind of useful health data, I would expect healthcare costs to drop and outcomes to improve.

It is easy to imagine other situations in which trading some privacy for larger benefits makes sense. And of course there will always be situations in which privacy is unambiguously good. I'll summarize it this way:

> If you think more privacy is always better, that is a case of loserthink. Every situation is different. Sometimes privacy is the problem that prevents the solution.

CHAPTER 6

Thinking Like an Engineer

PROFESSIONAL JEALOUSY

During my corporate career, I worked with a lot of engineers, program-mers, and other tech workers. That experience taught me a valuable lesson about how much to trust experts, and I thought it worth sharing.

I've been involved with dozens of software upgrade projects over the years, both in my cubicle days and later as a cartoonist and entre-preneur. And one thing you can always count on is that whoever is hired to work on the new version of the software will call the person who worked on the last version an idiot.

Let's label this phenomenon *professional jealousy*, although there are a

variety of motivations for mocking the last employee on the job. For example, mocking the last programmer is a good way to boost your perceived value, by comparing your awesomeness to the prior employee's uselessness. And the best part is that the target of your criticism is usually already gone and unable to defend against the charges. As a general rule, it's always smarter to criticize people who aren't around.

Assigning blame to the last person who worked on a project is not limited to technology workers. You see it in every job and in politics. And once you have seen it often enough, you can incorporate it into your thinking. And that means whenever you are talking to an expert in any realm, be aware that the next expert is likely to tell you the work done by the last expert looked like a monkey pounding a keyboard with a banana. And the expert after that will be just as rough on the prior expert, all the way to infinity. If experts are routinely skeptical of other experts, shouldn't you be skeptical of experts too?

I'm obviously exaggerating for effect, but I think you get the idea. For simple situations, experts usually agree. The problem comes with complicated situations in which there are opportunities for lots of judgment calls. And when I say experts, in this context I mean anyone with extra knowledge of a topic, including your coworkers.

If you are wondering how skeptical you should be about expert advice on complicated issues, keep in mind that the next expert probably has no respect for the last expert. And vice versa.

SEPARATING CAUSE AND SOLUTION

Engineers are trained to find practical solutions to problems even when emotions and politics are pushing untrained minds in the wrong direction. Non-engineers often find themselves locked in a mental prison that says the solution to a problem has to be tightly coupled with the cause. That can often be the right path. But sometimes the cause of a problem is not the best place to look for a solution, and engineers are trained to understand that. For example, there were 72,000 drug overdose deaths in the United States in 2017 alone. Some say the cause of the problem is the addicts themselves because no one is forcing them to take drugs. Therefore, say many observers, overdose deaths are solidly in the category of "not my problem."[1]

If you leave it to addicts to fix the opioid overdose problem on their own, you'll never have a solution. When the people who are at fault for a problem are unable or unwilling to fix it, your only choices are to live with the problem or find solutions unrelated to who is at fault. In the case of opioid addiction, that usually means government or charitable involvement to fund the recovery and treatment of addicts. When the annual number of deaths from opioids exceeds the number of American troops killed in Vietnam, Iraq, and Afghanistan combined, which is the current situation, it is the entire country's problem. Every overdose death leaves at least one family with permanent damage. Waiting for the addicts to solve the opioid problem because they are the ones "most responsible" for it is loserthink.

If your home were repeatedly burglarized, most of us would say the fault is with the criminals. But the solution might not involve criminals at all. The solution might involve, for example, getting a dog, better door locks, an alarm system, and an NRA sticker for your front door. Loserthink pairs the solution with the blame. A more productive way to think is that solutions can come from anywhere.

Consider the topic of immigration. The fault for illegal immigration lies entirely with the people who do it. But it isn't reasonable to expect they will be the ones who solve it. The only solutions to illegal immigration involve either the government making all immigration legal or finding better ways to keep people from immigrating to the country illegally.

Most people reading this book will prefer capitalism to pure socialism. And capitalism requires people to take personal responsibility for their financial success. Our legal system does the same. Society works best when people are held accountable for their own actions when it comes to money or the law. But it is a mistake to take the idea of personal accountability and apply it to every situation and every problem. Engineers are unlikely to make that sort of mistake. For them, the best solution can be independent of how we *feel* about the cause of the problem.

A common form of this loserthink is the "Who started it?" question. That's another way to assign responsibility. There are plenty of reasons to assign responsibility for outcomes, but it doesn't always tell you who is in the best position to solve the problem. If the group that started a problem is unable or unwilling to solve it, then the solution to the problem will be unrelated to the cause, and that's okay. Engineers learn to remove emotions from their decisions, and that allows them to find the best solution without being limited by the question of who is at fault.

The best solution to a problem is often unrelated to who is at fault. It is loserthink to believe otherwise.

If you have more than one child in your house, you might know how hard it is to get them to clean up after themselves when the easier path is for them to blame a sibling. For parents, it is loserthink to allow the "Who did it?" question to influence the decision about who cleans it up. My mother was a champion of this approach.

MOM: Scott, clean up the mess in the living room.

SCOTT: I didn't do that! It was Dave!

MOM: I didn't ask you who made the mess.

And then I cleaned up the living room. Mom didn't tolerate loser-think.

It is childlike thinking to insist in all cases that the people who cause problems are the only people who should solve them. A little bit of flexibility can go a long way.

ONE-VARIABLE ILLUSION

Engineers are trained to identify which combination of variables matters in a given situation. The thing that engineers know, and the general public often ignores, is that it is common for more than one variable to be important at the same time.

For most topics of national or global interest, you can't rely on bi-ased experts to sort things out for you, and those are the only experts you are likely to encounter. We generally have to rely on our own cleverness to discern truth from fake news. But how does one do that?

If you are like most people, you look for a one-variable shortcut. And sometimes that works. For example, years ago, when *Newsweek* was a physical magazine, they invited me to create a *Dilbert*-themed cover. The catch was that they were trying to decide between using my art versus another option in which they would use an attractive female face on the cover. I created the art, but I knew it was a waste of time. The one variable that mattered was that nearly all humans enjoy looking at attractive female faces. But perhaps 20 percent of the public would enjoy a *Dilbert*-themed comic. That's enough people to make me rich (and it did), but it can't compete with a cover that would be loved by nearly 100 percent of the public. As predicted, *Dilbert* did not appear on that cover. And in that case, one variable (an attractive female face) was predictive. But that is a special case. The more typical case is that you can't tell which variables are predictive.

After the 2016 election, pundits offered their opinions on why Hillary Clinton unexpectedly lost. If you have been alive for any full hour since then, chances are that you've heard dozens of explanations, mostly focusing on one variable or another. Some writers produced long lists of Clinton's missteps, as well as other "reasons" for her loss, in order to form a complete picture. But the loserthinkers, who were by far the majority, decided they could gaze into a situation that had hundreds of important variables and deduce "the one that mattered."

Rarely is an election decided by one variable. That is especially true in a presidential election. Hillary Clinton lost exactly the way she lost because *hundreds of variables were exactly what they were*. If any of those variables had been appreciably different, so too would the result. So when you find yourself saying Clinton lost because of one variable, be aware that you are talking nonsense. All the variables had to tip the way they did to get the result we got.[2]

If you analyze a complicated situation with multiple variables in play, and you conclude that only one of them was decisive, there's a good chance you are practicing loserthink.

You will be most tempted to default to one-variable thinking in the following situations in your life:

1. Figuring out why a relationship isn't working
2. Understanding the motivation of friends and family
3. Making business decisions in complicated situations

I don't know much about your particular life, so I will make my case using some topics we see in the news all the time. On the topic of climate change, for example, I often see skeptics declare that climate scientists will follow wherever the grant money leads them. Therefore, say the skeptics, we can't believe scientists who say the climate is warming to disastrous levels. Money does create massive bias, but it is simplistic to think it is the one variable you need to get to a rational opinion on climate science. Few things are as complicated and variable-rich as the topic of climate.

Other climate skeptics say climate change is a conspiracy by a group of elite globalists who are trying to destroy capitalism in favor of socialism. Once you know that, they say, you don't need to listen to the science. I dug into this belief a bit and learned it relies heavily on one misleading video clip taken out of context. But even if there were substance to the claim, it wouldn't explain why thousands of climate scientists around the world believe they are doing real science. Even cognitive dissonance and confirmation bias can't explain *all* of that.

On the topic of border security, we have observed since the election of 2016 that people are expressing one-variable opinions on opposite sides. The entire complexity of the topic comically shrunk down to "walls work" versus "walls don't work." Both opinions are ridiculous. Walls (or border barriers) are intended to create friction, change behavior, and perhaps reduce the need for human security in some areas. Complicating things further, a barrier that is good at slowing human traffic might be worthless for stopping drugs. Moreover, border barriers are more helpful in populated areas where illegal immigrants can disappear into a city on the other side. On barren lands with no nearby population centers, a low fence with sensors is all you need. If the sensors are tripped, border security shows up soon for the arrests because there is no good place to hide. A more nuanced opinion on border walls is that they create friction and change behavior, which border security experts say can be a helpful part of a larger mosaic of security solutions.

As a good general rule, simple situations can sometimes be predicted or explained by one key variable. But complicated situations, such as economies, climate change, and elections, are rarely one-variable situations.

CHAPTER 7

Thinking Like a Leader

Early in my career I thought I wanted to become a CEO, or at least a member of senior management somewhere. To learn the art of leadership, I went to school at night, worked a full-time job during the day, and earned my MBA degree from Berkeley. My coursework taught me how to analyze business and financial situations and make rational decisions. Unfortunately, there were no classes on persuasion, and persuasion is at least half of what a leader does all day. I learned persuasion on my own, and picked up other leadership skills over the years, mostly by observing people who did it right. Most of you know the basics of leadership, so I will focus on some concepts you are less likely to have seen.

THE DIRECTIONAL TRUTH FILTER

Let's say you hire a personal trainer who promises to get your body fat down from 35 percent to 15 percent. You work together for a few years and get your body fat down to 20 percent. Technically, your trainer was wrong. You might even say your trainer lied. But the trainer was directionally accurate, and you came out way ahead. Most of life is like this example. You can often know you are heading in the right direction, which matters a lot, while the precision of your estimates is secondary.

Truth has two important dimensions: 1) accuracy, and 2) direction. If you don't know which of those dimensions is more important, you might be in a mental prison.

If you are dealing with math, engineering, science, or medicine—to pick a few examples—you want your facts to be as accurate as possible. But even in those fields, it often matters more that you get the direction right.

For example, if an engineer determines that a new type of material would fail in one day under normal use, it doesn't matter too much if that estimate is wrong by a month. What matters is that the new material is unsuitable for daily use.

Likewise, a doctor might say that improving your diet will add twenty years to your life, even though you might live only another five years. The doctor is still directionally accurate in the sense that pursuing a better diet improves your odds of a healthy life.

You can probably think of examples in which you *do* need total precision in your facts, such as in engineering a product that meets specifications. But those situations are obvious when you see them.

We humans have a reflexive distaste for inaccuracy and lies. And we dislike people who traffic in such factual inaccuracies. That makes perfect sense, because we evolved as social creatures. Trust is the glue that holds social groups together. We are hardwired to prefer the truth.

The catch is that any leader who hopes to move the minds of the public will soon learn their facts and reason are poor tools for doing so. I describe this phenomenon more completely in my book *Win Bigly*. The gist of it is that humans are irrational creatures who mistakenly believe they use logic and reason to arrive at decisions. The reality, which science has proven in lots of different ways, is that we routinely make irrational decisions and then try to rationalize them. That's why the people who disagree with you so often appear to be not just wrong, but totally bonkers. And importantly, they think exactly the same about you.[1]

It's easy to tell when another person is rationalizing (as opposed to being rational), but it is nearly impossible to know when you are doing it yourself. That's why most of the social and political disagreements you see involve two or more idiots pointing at each other and screeching some form of "YOU IDIOT!" Both sides are right about the other being irrational, but wrong about themselves being rational.

A more productive way to see the world involves understanding that, for many types of truth, directional accuracy is all you need. For example, we might know that fair trade deals are better than unfair trade deals, but we don't know how much a particular change would improve the GDP. We just know better trade deals are better for the economy. We can know the right direction of that truth without knowing precisely how things will turn out.

The same is true for most political decisions. We often know which direction we need to head, but we typically don't know exactly where it will all end up. Getting the general direction right is critical, but being precisely accurate is only sometimes important.

If you find yourself complaining that a leader's claims are not passing the fact-checking, you might be technically correct. But your accurate observations won't necessarily matter in any important way. What will matter is whether or not that leader is persuading you and others in the right direction.

We all want to live in a world in which facts and reason, along with empathy and ethics, of course, influence our decisions, and nothing else gets in the way. But we don't live in that world. We do live in a world in which we can often know which direction we want things to move, but rarely can we know with any precision what we should do to get there, and how it will all turn out.

> If you find yourself obsessing over the accuracy of facts versus the direction those facts will lead you, you might be in a mental prison.

CONFUSING HYPERBOLE WITH LEGITIMATE OPINION

One of the most useful tools for any leader is something called hyperbole, better known as exaggeration. In the interest of persuasion, leaders typically exaggerate their strong points and understate their flaws. So if you want to understand what a leader really means, it helps to be able to sort the hyperbole from the facts.

In November 2018, House representative Eric Swalwell got into a Twitter exchange in which he noted that the government could enforce a ban on semiautomatic rifles—if such a law passed—because the government has lots of firepower compared to citizens. The conversation happened on Twitter, where creative exaggeration is normal, and Swalwell used some hyperbole to make his point. It did not go over well with proponents of the Second Amendment.

When I noticed the strong reaction on Twitter, I thought I could help clarify the situation by telling people that Swalwell's nuke reference

Joe Biggs ✓ @Rambobiggs · Nov 16
So basically @RepSwalwell wants a war. Because that's what you would get.
You're outta your fucking mind if you think I'll give up my rights and give the gov
all the power.

John Cardillo ✓ @johncardillo
Make no mistake, Democrats want to eradicate the Second Amendment,
ban and seize all guns, and have all power rest with the state.

These people are dangerously obsessed with power. ...

♡ 970   ⟲ 5.1K   ♡ 13K   ✉

Rep. Eric Swalwell ✓   (Follow)   ⌄
@RepSwalwell

Replying to @Rambobiggs

And it would be a short war my friend. The
government has nukes. Too many of them.
But they're legit. I'm sure if we talked we
could find common ground to protect our
families and communities.

12:22 PM - 16 Nov 2018

1,885 Retweets 1,786 Likes

was not the sort of thing one should take seriously, as it was clearly meant as hyperbole. I got two types of irrational responses to that opinion.

Irrational Response 1: This group said they understood the nuke reference to be hyperbole, but to them it signaled that Swalwell was suggesting the government could confiscate guns by threat of violence. That is accurate, but lacks the important context that the government enforces all major laws by threat of violence. That's how laws work. If you disobey any major law in this country, armed people paid by the government can find you and punish you. And if you use a weapon to resist that punishment, you can reasonably expect the government to use weapons to neutralize you.

If you try to build bombs or chemical weapons in your home, and the government finds out, they will send people with guns to fix that situation. Likewise, if the government passes legislation outlawing a certain type of gun, and let's say the Supreme Court agrees the law is constitutional, you can expect the government to use weapons to enforce that law too. So the idea that Swalwell was introducing a new draconian policy involving the government turning its weapons on citizens is completely off base. Swalwell was recommending a new law, and the government always uses guns to enforce major laws, either directly or indirectly. You can hate the law itself, but it's nonsense to debate the very nature of laws.

The legitimate question here is whether Swalwell's call to ban certain types of semiautomatic rifles is constitutional and desirable. I won't weigh in on that topic because it is outside the scope of this book. Instead, I will leave you with two lessons on loserthink. First:

> It is loserthink to take political hyperbole literally.

Irrational Response 2: This group said they knew all along that Swalwell was joking about the nukes, but they chose to *act* as if he meant it so they could "nail him," to get even for all the times Swalwell's team (Democrats) twisted the meaning of words on their team (Republicans). That isn't a productive plan.

> It is loserthink to attack an opponent by acting as dumb as they act. It might feel good, but it isn't a winning strategy.

SYSTEM VERSUS GOALS

Thomas Edison had a goal of inventing a practical light bulb. But his goal would have been useless without a system to achieve it. His system involved continuously testing different approaches until one of them worked. Had Edison been too specific about his goals, insisting on using one type of filament or developing one type of bulb, he would have failed. His system was permissive, in the sense that he didn't know what exact solution would be the best. He discovered the best solution by using his system.

Leaders understand that a good system involves doing something on a regular basis to improve your odds of good outcomes, even if you don't know exactly what the outcome will be.

For example, going to college and continuously learning new skills prepares you for lots of different opportunities, but you can't always predict where that will lead. If you develop good systems for improving your diet and fitness, that can help you in your health, personal life, and even career, but not in ways you can exactly predict.

One of my systems involves blogging and livestreaming on a variety of topics, then monitoring audience reaction to see where I should focus my energy. That system, which I have used for years, caused me to evolve from a cartoonist into a political pundit with a special focus on persuasion. There was no way I could have predicted that outcome. I simply continued adding skills to my skill stack while testing different messages and topics until something I was doing excited the audience. This was where it ended up.

As part of that journey, I built a large following on Twitter, and as a result got to see more examples of loserthink than I ever imagined possible. When I combined my new understanding of the most common forms of faulty thinking on social media with my writing skills and my general media skills, it brought you and me together over this book. None of this was predictable, except in the general sense that having good systems kicks up opportunities you wouldn't otherwise know existed.

When it comes to your personal life, business life, and political opinions, it makes sense to favor systems over goals whenever that is practical. A goal gives you one way to win, whereas a system can surface lots of winning paths, some of which you never could have imagined.

The loserthink trap here is that you often see people comparing political objectives and preferring one specific path to another. That sounds reasonable on the surface. But the smarter play would be to favor systems that give you lots of ways to win and a low chance of losing.

For example, in the United States we have lots of ideas for improving healthcare. And people talk about these various plans as if we should pick the best one and implement it. That is an example of bad thinking. The smarter approach is to admit we don't know which plans are the best and then find ways to test them small. Maybe one city or one small state wants to try it first. Ideally, different places would try different solutions so we someday are in a position to compare. Testing small and tracking results is a system. And it is one you are unlikely to criticize because it sounds so sensible.

Goals are for loserthinkers. Systems are for winners.

CHAPTER 8

Thinking Like a Scientist

COINCIDENCES

If you think your opinion on a topic is correct because of coincidences that can't be explained any other way, it might help you to know that confirmation bias looks exactly like that. We humans are terrible at knowing which coincidences are meaningful and which are just, well, coincidences. Luckily for us, scientists are trained to be skeptical of any kind of coincidence, and you would do well to follow their example.

The day I wrote this paragraph, I bought a package of Sharpies (marking pens), which I love using for a variety of reasons. While unpacking my shopping bag at home, my television was on, and I heard Greg Gutfeld proclaiming his love of Sharpies on the Fox News show *The Five*. That happened while I was holding my new Sharpies in my hand thinking how great they were. The world is bristling with meaningless coincidences.

Want some more?

A few days ago, I arranged my collection of flashlights on a display wall in my man cave that you might call my garage. I checked each flashlight and made sure the batteries were fresh. I love flashlights even more than I love Sharpies. The very next day, an SUV crashed into a power pole in my neighborhood and plunged my home into darkness for most of the evening hours. I believe this was the first time in ten years that my power had been out for so long at night. And it happened one day after I'd created a flashlight shrine so I would be prepared for this exact scenario.

Earlier that same day, I had a plumber fixing my shower. That evening, I watched a rerun of *Parks and Recreation* that included a scene in which a guy was fixing a shower. How often do I get my shower fixed? This was the first time I can remember in my entire life. And how often do you see someone on TV doing repairs on a shower? I can't recall one other time, but of course I would have no reason to remember it if I did.

In that same episode of *Parks and Recreation*, a subplot involved a guy living in a camping tent across the street from his ex so he could stalk her. I was watching the show with my girlfriend, Kristina, and by coincidence, one of her exes had actually stalked her by camping in a tent he'd pitched across the street. How weird is that?

Getting back to the plumber who fixed my shower, it was a big deal for me because I hadn't been able to use my own shower for a week. I couldn't wait to get back in that thing and experience its warm, wet embrace. I complained nonstop for a week to Kristina about not having my own shower. And when it was fixed, I could not have been happier. But before I could enjoy the awesomeness of my beloved shower, that SUV rammed the power pole and took out the power. Sometimes a power outage will damage electronic equipment. My house is bristling with electronics, and exactly one of them was damaged: the electronics for my water heater. I had exactly one major ambition for the week, which was to use my own shower, and by some extraordinary coincidence an SUV driver snatched away my chance at the worst possible time. What were the odds that the only two times my shower had ever had problems were back-to-back in the same week? And coincidentally, my water heater is a type my plumbers never work on, so they didn't have a way to get the part within days. So I ordered it from a supplier who promised to overnight it for early morning delivery. I was still waiting five days later.

Luckily, I had planned a writing trip that weekend, so I was in a hotel out of town. Which hotel, you ask? I didn't make the travel plans, but by coincidence I ended up in the same hotel I wrote about earlier in the book. But at least the table had no awkward tablecloth on it this time.

Today, on Twitter, someone sent around a viral video clip from a movie made in 1958 that involved a con man named Trump trying to sell a protective wall to unsuspecting villagers in a western town. At the same time I saw the video clip, President Trump was visiting the border to talk about his plans for a "wall." Politics aside, this was quite a coincidence.

Yesterday, I was taking calls on an app that my startup created called Interface by WhenHub. The app allows experts (at anything) to take video calls from people who are willing to pay for their time via the app. I set my price artificially low because I was promoting the app and wanted to guarantee I got calls. One of my callers was a young man who said he had read many of my books and was especially interested in the topic of affirmations, which I have written about a number of times. After reading my work, he decided he would try an affirmation aimed at finding a way to talk to me personally, so he could ask some follow-up questions about affirmations. When he saw my announcement on Twitter that I was live on the app, he quickly downloaded the app and connected with me. What were the odds that a motivated reader of my books would get to have a personal conversation with me while I sat on my couch at home? By coincidence, I cofounded a company that solved his exact problem of wanting to talk to me even though he had no access to my personal contact information.

Today, I opened on my computer the draft file of the book you are reading. I hadn't written a word for a few days and I needed to figure out where I'd left off last in my continuous rewrites. Luckily, the document was still open on my laptop to the place I'd left off. It was this section, titled "Coincidences." And my note to myself in the chapter was that I needed to add some examples of coincidences. Entirely by coincidence, a number of recent coincidences were fresh in my mind, and you have just read them. This was an easy section to complete.

What do all these coincidences mean? Absolutely nothing. Coincidences happen all the time. But we humans are wired to put meaning on coincidences, and when we do, we are often engaged in loserthink.

To be fair, sometimes coincidences do mean something. If the police are investigating a domestic murder, and the surviving spouse booked a flight out of the country right before it happened, that might not be a coincidence at all. But the far more typical situation is when we think a coincidence means something and it doesn't. We are surrounded by coincidences. Most mean nothing at all.

The most common situations in which coincidences can be misleading involve your career and your personal life. When the topic has an emotional element, and you are already primed to believe something to be true, expect the environment to serve up lots of false signals.

For example, if you suspect a romantic partner of lying, suddenly you see signs of it everywhere, even if those signals are false. And if you think a particular plan in your workplace is a bad one, you will see all kinds of signals you are right, even when you are not. The more you care about a topic, the more susceptible you are to assigning meaning to coincidences. And if the situation is rich with variables, you will have plenty from which to choose.

Sometimes coincidences tell you something useful. But 90 percent of the time they mislead you. Never be too confident about an opinion that depends solely on interpreting a coincidence.

ANECDOTAL EVIDENCE

One of the most common forms of loserthink involves treating individual situations as though they represent an overall pattern or trend. When this sort of observational "evidence" is in play, the term for it is *anecdotal*, meaning it comes from your unstructured observations as opposed to scientific or other credible data. And therefore it should not be deemed persuasive.

If someone wearing a green hat punches you in the stomach, you might irrationally draw the conclusion that green-hat-wearing people are dangerous. If you are smart, you'll realize this is nothing but anecdotal evidence and not representative of all wearers of green hats. In our everyday life, most people understand the difference between anecdotal evidence and scientific evidence. But . . .

The problem occurs when the media slants its coverage of stories so you see what you believe to be a pattern. If every story on your preferred news source focuses on green-hatted violence, you will quickly come to believe it is a big problem. I just described every news outlet. They all focus on the stories and images that support their political leanings. And that focus on stories, usually involving death or danger, gives the consumer a slanted impression. This is especially true for news coverage of anything involving violence. If all we see are news articles about punchy green-hatted people, we will soon come to believe they are the biggest menace to society.

If you are reaching a general conclusion about a big topic by looking at anecdotal evidence, you are engaging in loserthink.

ASK YOURSELF: "WHAT IF THE OPPOSITE IS TRUE?"

German mathematician Carl Gustav Jacob Jacobi—whose parents were not good at naming babies—was known for his maxim that it is often easier to solve a problem if you express it as its opposite.[1]

Famous investor Charlie Munger, best known as Warren Buffett's business partner, uses a version of this method to look at investments; instead of asking how they might succeed, he first tries to understand what failing would look like in this situation, and how to avoid it.[2]

As a cartoonist, one of my writing techniques involves considering common situations and asking myself what it would look like if my assumptions were exactly backward. For example, we assume our doctors want to heal us and they try hard to do so. But for comic purposes, it is funnier to imagine the opposite, that the doctor is a serial killer who found a legal way to pursue his hobby. Now all he does is dispense bad medical advice. I do this mental exercise of reversing reality often as part of my work, and so I reflexively do it with topics I see in the news, my personal life, and everywhere else. Usually, things are not the opposite of how they look, but it helps to be on the lookout for times when that is the case.

Have you ever suspected a loved one was trying to do something bad to you and later discovered they were trying to do you a favor? If you lock yourself into the first theory before discovering you are wrong, much damage can be done before you learn the truth. But if your first reflex is to ask yourself what if the opposite of the first impression is true, you're on safer ground. Often it helps to hold both your suspicion and the opposite of your suspicion as equally possible until you know for sure.

The way human minds are wired, if we take a firm position on a topic, we are unlikely to change our minds even when facts emerge that debunk our initial belief. That's why it is smarter to not commit to a firm opinion when facts are still coming into focus. My mantra in these situations is: But I could be totally wrong. That gives me the mental freedom to later adjust my opinion if needed.

Always ask yourself if the opposite of your theory could be true. Doing so keeps you humble and less susceptible to bias until you get to the truth of the situation.

JUDGING A GROUP BY ITS WORST MEMBERS

Scientists are trained to understand that stories and observations can be persuasive at the same time they are misleading, which is a dangerous situation. We nonscientists are easily influenced by individual stories, especially when they include bad behavior from members of any group.

As I write this book, Democrats are accusing Republicans of being racists because some of them are. Meanwhile, Republicans are accusing Democrats of being socialists, criminals, and anarchists because some of them are.

If your intention is to win at all costs, this sort of unethical branding of the other side can work wonders. If you do it right, you can convince your team to hate those outsiders with a passion that borders on violence. Don't do that, please.

If you find yourself believing that several million people in your own country share a common set of despicable traits, despite overwhelming evidence to the contrary, you might be engaging in loserthink that will make you less happy and less effective.

If you are genuinely trying to understand the world, please avoid judging entire groups by their worst members. It's bad enough that people on your own team encourage you, by example, to think that way. But if you copy that kind of loserthink, I don't recommend feeling proud of it.

The business model of the free press depends on reinforcing the ideas that each side of the political divide in the United States is as bad as the worst 5 percent. That creates endless news stories in which minor events get reframed as the entire group's bad behavior. Keep that in mind when reading stories about how one group or the other is "always doing X."

Don't believe that every member of a group is as bad as its worst 5 percent. If you do, you're probably among the worst 5 percent of whatever groups you are in.

PROVING A NEGATIVE

If any part of your argument depends on asking critics to "prove it isn't true," you are thinking like a cult member. Generally speaking, it isn't possible to prove things don't exist. The best you can do is show that you can't detect the existence of something. But that is very different from proving something can't be done or doesn't exist. Here's an example of my California representative, Eric Swalwell, challenging the public to prove a negative, which of course is impossible.

Can I prove my decisions are not being directed by an advanced species of space aliens who are using a brain-gun to influence me without my knowledge? No, I can't prove it isn't happening. But that doesn't mean it *is* happening.

I mentioned the Q conspiracy theory earlier. Believers in Q swarmed my Twitter feed after I said Q wasn't real and challenged me to "prove Q isn't really a Deep State insider like he claims." I don't think it is an accident that members of the Q cult do not understand that one cannot prove a negative. I can, and did, point them to links showing Q does

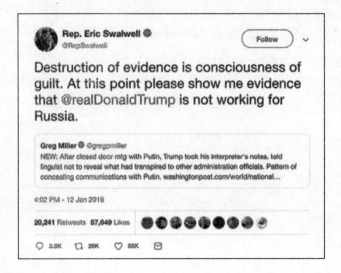

not accurately predict the future. At that point, the Q followers re-treated to some nonsense about Q teaching people to research for themselves, as some sort of excuse for why the predictions are more wrong than right. It seems to me that Q followers, or at least most of them, have not studied any of the disciplines that teach one how to think. And I say that with love, as I think the followers of Q have good intentions. But if they have never been exposed to the disciplines that teach one how to think effectively, they might be at a disadvantage in deducing the truth of Q.

People who are trained in decision-making know it is not rational to ask someone to prove a negative. So if you find yourself demanding that others do so, you are practicing loserthink.

> Rarely is it possible to prove something isn't true. But sometimes we can prove things are true.

CHAPTER 9

Thinking Like an Entrepreneur

COUCH LOCK

I'm a trained hypnotist, and that experience has completely changed how I see the world. As a hypnotist, you rewire people's minds in real time, as if they are what I call "moist robots." If you haven't personally witnessed a mind being rewired, it would be hard for you to release any romantic notions you might have about humans as independent souls with free will. For our purposes here, I won't get into the philosophy of it all; I will simply suggest that understanding how hypnotists think about the programmability of human brains can be useful in a variety of settings. You don't need to "believe hypnosis is real" in order to take advantage of the thinking style that emerges from that practice. Just try the method I describe below and see for yourself if it gives you a good result.

Lazy people and stoners have a term that describes how it feels when they can't motivate themselves to get off the couch. It's called *couch lock*. Your body is presumably *able* to get off the couch, and perhaps you *want* to get up, but you lack the specific motivation. It feels as if you are trapped in your own lazy body.

You don't have to smoke marijuana to experience couch lock. We've all experienced times when we wanted to get up and do something useful but we couldn't talk ourselves into it. It can happen when you are tired, unmotivated, shy, anxious, or even depressed. Your body sits there like a bag of potatoes while your helpless brain thinks that getting up and doing something would be a good idea. For some mysterious reason, your brain can't give the order to your body to make it get off the couch. You might know you need to make a phone call or take a class to further your life ambitions, but for some reason you don't do it. Maybe you think you know why, and maybe you don't. But the net result is that your brain can't force your body to do the simple things you know you need to do to improve your situation. For all practical purposes, you're locked in a mental prison of your own making.

Even if you don't have a couch-related problem, you might feel paralyzed in major areas of your life. Are you thinking about changing jobs, applying to graduate school, moving someplace better, learning a new skill, or upgrading your love life? Your first step is figuring out how to cure your own impulse for inaction.

The secret to thwarting couch lock of any sort is to stop imagining everything you *need* to do, and start imagining the *smallest step* that you *can* do without much real effort. If you feel you can't talk yourself into standing up and doing something that needs to get done, talk yourself into moving your pinky finger. Then move it.

As you move your pinky, you will immediately regain the sense of agency over your body that had been temporarily missing. Moving your pinky finger is easy no matter how stoned, tired, depressed, or unmotivated you are. Do what you *can* do, not what you *can't*. Then build on the momentum.

What you will quickly learn is that moving your pinky finger makes it easy to wiggle the other fingers. Then you can easily move your hand, your arm, and the rest of your body. You'll be off the couch in about ten seconds.

A similar approach works for those big things you need to do in life that you can't talk yourself into doing. Figure out the smallest step you can take and then do it. Then take the next microstep. Stop thinking about the whole project you have in mind, as that will overwhelm you and stun you into couch lock. Just do what you can easily do, and watch how quickly that action makes it easier to do the next action.

Sometimes I experience "phone lock." That happens when I know I need to call someone but I can't force myself to pick up the phone and do it. I give myself one excuse after another about why it's okay not to act right now. The solution is to do what you *can* do, which might include writing a to-do list with that item at the top. Or maybe you need to find the phone number first, so do that part and allow yourself the permission to stop there. When your brain is experiencing any kind of couch-lock situation, figure out the first microstep in your desired pathway that is simple enough that you are willing to do it. Even if that microstep is nothing more than wiggling a pinky finger.

In 1988, I decided to pivot from my stalled corporate career to become a cartoonist. But how does one become a cartoonist? Where do you start? What do you do first? I had no idea. The enormity of the challenge was a huge mental obstacle. So I did the smallest task I could talk myself into doing. I drove to the local art supply store and bought some high-quality pens and paper for drawing. That was all I did that day to begin working on my long-term career objective.

Later that week, I sat down with my pens and paper and started doodling, mostly to test the quality of the materials and to see how much I liked them. And that was all I did that day.

I decided to set my alarm clock half an hour earlier than normal from that day on so I would have time to draw some comics, for practice, and drink coffee before work. That became my morning ritual. Each step was tiny, but they added up. By 1989, I had assembled enough microsteps to get exactly where I wanted to be. That year, Dilbert started running in newspapers across the country.

Looking back, I see the amount of effort I put into becoming a cartoonist was enormous. But on any particular day, the effort was quite manageable. And that's how life works in lots of realms. We take continuous microsteps that sum up to big things over time.

I just freed you from couch lock. But you won't know it until the first time you remember this chapter and find yourself wiggling your pinky to start something you need to do.

Loserthink involves imagining the entire task ahead and letting it stun you into inaction. The opposite of loserthink is breaking down a big task into the tiniest step you are willing to do right now. Then build from there, one tiny task at a time.

Learn to think in microsteps. If you are experiencing couch lock, try wiggling one finger. Then build from there.

Hypnotists and entrepreneurs have overlapping thinking styles when it comes to motivating themselves to take action. When entrepreneurs don't know how to get from A to B, they take the smallest step in that direction that is available to them and then see if they can figure out the next one from that new starting point. Hypnotists who see humans as programmable entities understand that they have to start with small suggestions, such as "Your eyelids feel heavier," in order to work up to larger actions, such as "Your arm is so light it will start to float." When the hypnotist succeeds at the smaller suggestions, it primes the subject to be receptive to larger suggestions, such as lifestyle changes or getting past a phobia. When you wiggle your pinky to escape couch lock, you are acting like both the hypnotist and the subject, and you quickly realize the small suggestions to yourself prime you to take bigger actions, and it happens almost immediately.

STAYING IN YOUR LANE

At the time of this writing, the two most influential politicians in the United States are a real estate developer who became president and a bartender who got elected to Congress. For those of you reading this book a few decades from now, I'm talking about President Trump and Representative Alexandria Ocasio-Cortez. The most striking thing they have in common is that they did not "stay in their lanes," and it worked out great for them.

Likewise, you would not be reading this book, and the Dilbert comic strip would not exist, if I had "stayed in my lane," which at the time meant working in a cubicle.

My nomination for the most loserthinkish advice in history is: "Stay in your lane." That is the sort of advice that is better served to an enemy, not a friend. If everyone followed that advice, you wouldn't have civilization. The world as we know it was engineered, designed, and built by people who left their lane and tried something outside their temporary skill stack. They figured it out as they went.

I'll agree that one size doesn't fit all, and some people probably should stick to what they do best. But I wouldn't want society to decide that staying in one lane is some sort of obvious wisdom. In my experience, the smartest plan for life is to leave your lane as often as you can (without inviting major risk) to pick up skills that will complement your talent stack. The more skills you have, the more valuable you will be, although you won't necessarily know in advance where it will take you.

If you happen to be one of the best in the world at some specific skill, such as sports, music, or science—and you like what you do—it might make perfect sense to "stay in your lane" and milk that situation for all it is worth. But most of us are not the best in the world, or anywhere near it, at any particular skill. If that describes you, I recommend leaving your lane often—even at the risk of embarrassment—to pick up new skills and new ways to see the world. Here's a list of skills I have sampled, as opposed to mastered, over my lifetime:

Economics	Negotiating
Business	Budgeting and finance
Management	Persuasion
Sales	Entrepreneurship
Psychology	Marketing
Hypnosis	Publishing
Programming	Social media
Commercial lending	Video editing
Project management	Photoshop
Public speaking	Engineering
Design	Drumming
Art	Cartooning
Writing	Political punditry
Television production	Livestreaming

The best way to widen your lane is to leave it often, so you can learn something new. I prefer picking projects in which I will come out ahead no matter what kind of luck I have. If I learn some useful new skills, and I make some valuable contacts, and I learn to see the world through the filter of the new skill, I know I have become more valuable and my lane has widened.

Leaving your lane and learning a new skill can be deeply rewarding. The experience of struggling to learn a new skill and then mastering it over time can be a big boost to your confidence. And it is the best way to remind yourself you can prevail in hard situations. Two of my favorite sentences are . . .

1. I don't know how to do that.
2. But I can figure it out.

Learning to take sensible chances outside your lane is one of the best life skills you will ever acquire. And it is available to all of us.

> Sticking with what you know ensures you stay where you are. Take some chances. Leave your lane and build some skills.

PERSONAL CONTROL

One of the fringe benefits of being mildly famous is that I meet a lot of successful entrepreneurs. I also know lots of people who have failed so often it seems intentional. If I had to pick one defining characteristic that separates the successful from the unsuccessful, it would be luck.

But if I had to pick two defining characteristics, the other one would be a sense of control. Successful people, and people who will someday be successful, seem to believe they can steer their fate by their actions.

Whether they are right about that or not, it's a winning mindset. People who think they control their situations will put more effort into doing so.

In 2013, my book *How to Fail at Almost Everything and Still Win Big* came out. By 2014, I was getting messages from readers telling me how they had used the tips in the book to radically improve their careers, health, and personal lives. The book teaches readers how to create easy systems that improve their odds of success. Evidently, it had a big impact on people who tried it out. Perhaps the most important thing the book does is move people's minds from wondering how to succeed in a world that seems mostly driven by luck, to habit-driven systems in which you are evolving from a situation with low odds of finding luck to situations with better odds. When you spend time every day doing something productive, whether that involves learning something useful or exercising, for example, you gain a sense of control over your reality. And that sense of control can be both motivating and satisfying, which helps you do more of what works.

At the other extreme, people who are consistently unsuccessful often believe they are victims of life, although the details of that victimhood can differ. Think of the people you know who are consistently late for everything. Do they blame themselves? Sometimes, yes. But usually they tell you traffic was bad or something came up that was out of their control.

Now talk to the people who are always five minutes early no matter what. That group believes timeliness is about 90 percent under their control. And that kind of belief is a strong predictor of success.

You can figure out which group you are in by asking yourself what is keeping you from achieving your objectives in life. Is the first answer that comes to mind something about your own efforts? Or did you immediately think about an obstacle that life has put in your way? If you take full responsibility for your outcomes, even while knowing much of it depends on luck, that's how rich people think. If you blame something beyond your direct control, you're probably engaged in loserthink, and your outcomes will reflect it.

Now let me talk directly to the people who would like to be successful in life but are "thinking like poor people." And by that I mean you believe you are not the primary authors of your own life experience. The place to start is by changing that mindset. If you don't fix that first, don't expect anything else to work out for you. I think nearly every successful person would agree with me on this point: get your mind right first. Everything else depends on that.

The simple way to learn how to think like a rich person is to start reading books on the topic. And your first microstep on that path is to buy one or more of those books and have them in your home or on your digital device for when you are ready to consume them. Don't think about reading a book (which might seem hard). Think about buying a book, which can be as simple as one-click online ordering. Once you have the book, think in terms of reading one page or one chapter at a time. Put it in your bathroom if that helps. Put it on your phone if it is an ebook, and make it a habit to read a chapter anytime you are waiting in line. Take microsteps. And if you like what you got out of the first book, repeat. There are plenty of super-helpful books on how to get your mind right for success.

I recommend one of my own books as a starter: *How to Fail at Almost Everything and Still Win Big*. If I may ignore modesty here in the interest of being useful, people who read that book consistently report that it improved their lives by improving their mental game. But you don't need to trust the author of the book. Just read the customer reviews and ignore the ones from people who seem to be mad at me for unrelated stuff. The main theme of the book is about how to think of your path to success as a series of systems instead of goals.

Other notable authors in the getting-your-mind-right genre are Tony Robbins, Tim Ferriss, James Altucher, Seth Godin, and Mike Cernovich. I recommend any book by them.

You can learn to think like a rich person by consuming books, blog posts, and podcasts from the authors who can teach you how. If this sort of reading isn't your thing, make it your thing, one micro-step at a time.

HUMILITY AND TESTING

Confidence is a great quality to have, unless you're also often wrong. In that case, you've got two strikes against you: you're wrong and you're an arrogant jerk with too much confidence. That's not a good look.

If you happen to be a human being—and many of my readers are—you are wrong about all sorts of things more often than you admit, and more often than you remember. Obviously you're not as wrong as other people you know. Other people are a mess. I think we can agree on that. But as wonderful as you are compared to them, you probably have some blind spots too when it comes to understanding the world.

Nature was kind enough to grant us imperfect brains that easily forget most of the situations in which we have been confident about our rightness only to later find out we were impressively wrong. I, for one, am glad nature gave us this ego-saving amnesia about our frequent mistakes. If we knew how often we were wrong about our understanding of just about everything, it would be deeply demotivating. And if we become demotivated, the portal to progress will shut tighter than a mosquito's nozzle* in an ice storm.

As I write this chapter, I'm having a Twitter debate with climate change skeptics who fervently believe climate scientists are ignoring the impact of sun activity when they study global warming. I don't think you need to be a climate expert to know that those who study the climate for a living did not forget THE FRICKING SUN. Believing they forgot the sun would be like believing scientists who study the health impact of owning pets forgot to consider dogs. My certainty that climate scientists have considered all aspects of the sun on global warming is matched only by the certainty of the skeptics who insist they haven't. Certainty isn't a good indication of rightness for any complicated situation. As evidence of that point, consider anyone who disagrees with you on any topic whatsoever. They are as confident as you are. And you can't both be right.

Perhaps you think I'm exaggerating about how often people are confident in their opinions while at the same time they are hilariously wrong. After all, how could so much human wrongness produce our modern world?

Luckily for us, the scientific method is more reliable than human certainty, and it allows for a lot of failure, so long as *some* things turn out to be right. Most experiments fail. Many published scientific papers turn out to be wrong, or at least imperfect. But you only need a small percentage of rightness in all of that science to move society forward. It doesn't matter how many times science is wrong so long as sometimes it is right and the good stuff sticks around. To put it in sporting terms, no one cares how many fish you *didn't* catch. They only care about the

---

* I think mosquitoes have nozzles. Possibly beaks. Or snouts. I don't know a lot about bugs.

ones you did. (Unless they are judging your fish-catching efficiency, which would be a different topic.)

Capitalism is similar to both science and fishing in that it is largely a failure machine. Most startups fail, for example, and most companies eventually go out of business, one way or another. But while all that failing is happening, employees are getting paid, vendors are selling products and services to the doomed business while it lasts, and the economy chugs along. You only need a small percentage of companies to succeed in order to have a strong economy.[1]

You might be tempted to think successful companies all have smart founders who see the world clearly, and that skill set is what helps them succeed. But the reality is that entrepreneurs are making educated guesses and talking themselves into a degree of certainty that the facts do not support. People buck the odds because they don't believe those odds apply to their situations. And it's a good thing this sort of irrationality exists, because otherwise people wouldn't take risks and the economy would fall apart.

Being wrong and yet confident is a good description of the human condition. And it isn't hard to understand why we are this way. Our consistent wrongness has a lot to do with the fact that the world is a complicated place and it is hard to predict what will happen next. Yet we are continually forced to predict the future in both big and small ways because otherwise we wouldn't know what we should be doing at any given moment. We get the easy stuff right, such as knowing we'll want a beverage if we eat pretzels. But when it comes to the big, complicated, long-term predictions, we're not equipped with the psychic powers required to know how the future turns out. We also can't stop ourselves from imagining we do know how things will work out. I'm not the exception. Neither are you.

Our irrational confidence makes sense if you assume humans evolved to have traits that help us survive. Our world rewards action over inaction, at least in the average sense. The entrepreneur who tries ten startups has a reasonable chance of making it big with at least one. But the person who doesn't try anything at all is unlikely to succeed. As a general rule, people have to go find luck; it doesn't find them. Luck is attracted to action and energy; it doesn't come looking for you on the couch.

One big disadvantage of being both confident and wrong is that we construct artificial worlds in our minds that are based on that wrongness. We are confident we can discern which news reports are real and which are not. We are confident we know how to hire good employees. We are confident our scientific studies tell us something useful, until new studies fail to confirm what we thought we knew. We are confident the people we marry will love us forever. Most of us are confident our opinions on religion are correct while believing that everyone who has a different religious opinion is wrong. And if you are an investor, there are probably times when you are sure you can see the future, at least for the companies in which you've invested. But that confidence is generally not fact-driven.

When we combine our irrational certainty on all sorts of topics with our normal human capacity to be spectacularly wrong, we end up with a civilization in which people have designed elaborate mental prisons for themselves. We all inhabit a reality of our own making. In each of our artificial realities, we know our version of things is both proper and right, while all the people who disagree with us are obviously wretched, ignorant, and weak. Sometimes we feel sorry for them.

Most of the time it doesn't matter who is right and who is wrong. You can be failing at your science experiment and also in your marriage while I'm failing in business and gullibly consuming one conspiracy theory after another. And yet, despite all of our wrongness, both of us can eat, sleep, and procreate. Nature doesn't seem to care whether we are smart. In terms of our survival as a species, it only matters that some people, in some places, get things right some of the time. And if that success comes only from luck, that still moves society forward.

Favoring action over inaction, even in the face of uncertainty, is generally a good approach to life. The world rewards energy, and it even rewards failure by teaching you valuable lessons and expanding your network of contacts.

One form of loserthink is having too much confidence in your own rightness and your ability to divine the future. Another form of loserthink involves waiting too long to develop confidence in your worldview before acting. It might seem as if there are only two options in life—do something or do nothing—and both paths have a high chance of failing. So what do you do?

For the solution to that dilemma, I borrow from the fields of science, business management, and entrepreneurship for a better way to think. And they provide the answer. It goes like this:

Find a way to test your assumption in a small way so no one gets hurt.

Those of you with backgrounds in the fields I just mentioned reflexively think in terms of testing things small before going big. But the vast majority of the public has no education in those disciplines. For them, loserthink is the default approach because they have never learned any other way. They either recklessly insist on starting big (unrealistic confidence) or they favor doing nothing at all (failure by inaction). If that describes you, I just fixed it for you. You only have to be exposed to the idea of testing things small before committing to something big. And it is immediately obvious why that makes sense, at least whenever it is practical to do so.

The next time you find yourself in a debate about doing something big, ask yourself how the idea can first be tested small. The alternatives are loserthink.

CHAPTER 10

Thinking Like an Economist

MONEY INFLUENCE

As a teenager, I observed the world around me and I often didn't understand why people did what they did. This was before I learned that human beings are fundamentally irrational creatures. The one thing of which I was certain, both from observation and personal experience, was that money motivates people. I thought that if I could understand the field of economics, I would have a huge advantage in comprehending my world. When it came time for college, I made economics my major. In my late twenties, I went back to school for evening classes and earned a master's in business administration (MBA) from the Haas School of Business at the University of California at Berkeley. Both of those educational experiences confirmed my hypothesis that understanding economics helps you understand the world on a deeper level.

For instance, I use my understanding of economics to avoid speeding tickets. The police department is like any organization that has a limited budget and limited resources. It is fair to assume that they have figured out how to get the most enforcement value out of the dollars they have. And that means not wasting resources handing out speeding tickets on Sunday mornings at six a.m., for example. It wouldn't make economic sense to deploy resources when there is so little traffic. One of the benefits of giving out speeding tickets is that the other motorists see it happen. You don't get that benefit with one motorist and one police officer on an empty highway.

It's probably also harder to find law enforcement employees who would be willing to work the odd hours. It might even cost more because of supply and demand.

Like nearly everyone else who drives, I sometimes exceed the speed limit. But I use my knowledge of economics to predict when and where the police—with their limited budget and resources—are likely to have speed traps. Obviously, my method is not 100 percent effective, but watch how rarely you see speed traps on off hours of the week. And please don't drive unsafely.

> A basic understanding of economics can help you "see around corners" that others cannot.

Sometimes people who don't understand economics will tell me they plan to buy real estate and rent it out to make money. Without doing any research whatsoever, I tell them with confidence that such opportunities do not exist in my state. My economic reasoning is that real estate brokers buy those properties as soon as they are available (which is rare), so the rest of the public never sees them. How do I know that? It's obvious if you understand economics. I've also done the math to confirm that these opportunities do not exist in any common way. But if you talk to experienced real estate brokers, there's a good chance they own a few rental properties. They buy what you never get a chance to see. If the properties have positive cash flow, why wouldn't one of the brokers who view properties before the general public buy it for themselves? They would, and they do, exactly as I assumed. My knowledge of business and economics made this obvious to me from the start. When you understand the world of money, and you understand human nature, it feels as if you can see around corners.

People who understand economics can more easily spot hoaxes because money drives human behavior in predictable ways.

I once talked to a professional financial advisor who recommended managed stock funds for his clients. The funds he recommended paid him to recommend their firms, so his clients were not getting independent advice. They were getting conned. They paid this advisor about 1 percent of their portfolio per year to park their money with another fund that also charged a management fee. None of those fees added value. And the financial advisor knew this. I asked him where he put his own money, and he laughed, saying he put his own money in unmanaged index funds that anyone could buy without paying fees to experts who recommend them. I already knew the answer to my question because I understand human nature, I know enough about investing, and I knew how the expert could make the most money.

In the case of the financial advisor, everything he was doing was legal, although one could argue it shouldn't have been. One of the most consistent rules of life is that bad behavior happens almost 100 percent of the time whenever you have this combination of variables:

1. There is money to be made from the bad behavior
2. The odds of detection are low
3. Lots of people are involved

When you have that setup, it is reasonable to assume crime is rampant. Unfortunately, I just described much of the financial world. Consider insider trading, for example. If you do it in a dumb way, you are likely to get caught. But there are plenty of ways to avoid detection, the potential gains are huge, and lots of people have access to insider information. And sure enough, insider trading is a common crime.

Your best defense for navigating a world in which experts are too often frauds is to seek second opinions whenever that is an option. Real experts are likely to give you advice that is similar or at least compatible. Frauds are more likely to freelance, meaning any two frauds would give you different advice. And whenever possible, ask a retired expert or a family friend for a second opinion. The frauds of this world always have an advantage, but if you are alert to the influence of money, you can spot them more easily.

> Be skeptical of any experts who have a financial incentive to mislead you and almost no risk on their end.

ENDS JUSTIFY THE MEANS

Economists learn how to make rational comparisons of alternatives. This skill is not common among the general public, and it shows. For example, people often ask me if the ends justify the means, on all sorts of topics, usually political. You have probably seen that question on social media as well as heard it from the punditry class. The question is an attempt to win a debate before the debate happens. It's a clever word trap, designed to paint you as immoral if you stick to your original opinion.

A similarly tricky question is, "Do you still abuse your spouse?" There is no right answer to that question. If you say yes, you're a spouse abuser. If you say no, you have admitted you were once a spouse abuser.

When people ask you if the ends justify the means, they are trying to frame themselves as the moral player in the conversation while framing you as the unethical weasel. Don't answer the trick question. Instead, restate the question in this form before answering: I think you mean: Are the benefits greater than the costs?

After reframing the question, explain that a good decision-maker considers all the relevant costs and all the benefits, including moral and ethical considerations. We live in a social world in which ethics and morality matter, in terms of how we feel about ourselves and our place in the universe, as well as in a practical sense, meaning that you might be setting a bad example, creating a bad precedent, or inviting problems you don't want. All of those considerations are part of the cost-benefit analysis.

I just described the polite way to answer, "Do the ends justify the means?" The funny version goes like this: "I consider all the costs and all the benefits of my decisions, including the moral and ethical questions. What do you do?"

Suppose I asked you if you would lie to a terrorist to thwart a terror attack. Lying is generally considered unethical, but in this specific case, the benefits clearly outweigh the costs.

On the other extreme, suppose I said I wanted to shoot someone because I didn't like that person's haircut. Nearly everyone reading this book believes the cost of doing that would exceed the benefits on all the important dimensions, legally, practically, and morally. When people consider all the costs and all the benefits of a decision, including the ethical/moral considerations, we might disagree with their conclusions, but not the process by which they were formed. A trained economist would know to consider all factors in a decision. The public at large tends to leave out the parts they don't like.

If you reframe the "ends justify the means" question as a balance of costs and benefits, expect the target of your persuasion to respond with some sort of Hitler/murderer analogy in which the benefits do not exceed the costs on any dimension. The best response to a bad analogy is to say you don't address analogies because those are different situations by definition, but you would be happy to address the costs and benefits around your topic.

> If you think in terms of "the ends justifying the means" instead of "costs compared to benefits," you are buying into loserthink.

HOW TO COMPARE THINGS

As I mentioned, I was an economics major in college. Later I went on to get my MBA. Those college courses taught me, among other things, how to compare alternatives in a rational way. If you have not learned

that skill, and you mistakenly believe it is "common sense," you are at a tremendous disadvantage in all dimensions of life, from your career to your opinions on politics.

Medical professionals also learn how to compare things. For example, a *differential diagnosis* involves determining the probability a patient has one type of illness versus others and then picking a treatment plan that offers the best balance of risks and likely outcomes.

Engineers and other professionals also learn how to compare options in the most rational way. When I deal with people who have come from any of those disciplines, I find I am talking the same language and we can often follow the same fact-path from assumptions all the way to conclusions. And when we disagree, we can easily identify which variable or assumption caused the difference. That allows us to do a deeper dive on the source of disagreement to see if we can find common ground.

TWO ECONOMISTS DEBATING

ECONOMIST 1: This analysis is misleading because it ignored the stronger alternative.

ECONOMIST 2: What is the stronger alternative?

ECONOMIST 1: Here's a link to a description of it.

ECONOMIST 2: I see your point. You're right.

See how civil that was? Now compare that exchange to two non-economists debating exactly the same topic.

TWO NON-ECONOMISTS DEBATING

PERSON 1: That idea is stupid.

PERSON 2: Why?

PERSON 1: Well, for starters, you are a globalist who wants to destroy the world to make it safe for trees.

PERSON 2: I'm a Republican.

PERSON 1: I meant to say racist.

I'm exaggerating a bit for effect, but my experience has been that debating with someone who understands economics is a civilized encounter even if you end up disagreeing in the end. And two economists would likely isolate the point of disagreement—a fact in dispute, for example—and commit to researching that fact further. Non-economists usually go in a different direction.

Obviously there are non-economists who have also learned how to compare things rationally. I would expect to find the largest number of them in the fields of science, technology, and business. Art majors, for comparison, probably don't spend a lot of time learning how to rigorously compare alternatives.

So where does that leave the 90 percent of the population who have not studied the art of comparing things? In my experience, it leaves them believing they do have that skill while I observe that they do not.

The skill one needs for comparing things is similar in a sense to any other human skill. The people who have been taught to do it right, and the people who have practiced it over time, are going to be a lot better at it than people who are just winging it. Learning a new skill and practicing it is a system that works for just about any talent you can describe.

For most other types of skills, we are completely aware of our limited capabilities compared to those who have been trained. For example, I know I shouldn't get in a fight with someone who has a black belt in karate. I know I shouldn't get in a debate about statistics with a professional statistician. But if I had never been formally educated in "comparing things," I probably wouldn't even know it was a skill that could be improved. And if I don't know it is a learned skill, I probably think I am good at it already. That kind of blind spot can become a wall in your mental prison.

To bring you up to speed on how to compare things, I will describe some basic concepts. You might find yourself saying you already understand everything I am about to explain even though you have not been formally trained in decision-making. But I submit to you that knowing how to read music and knowing which keys on the piano correspond to those notes does not make you a musician. Music, like decision-making, has to be practiced in a rigorous fashion for years before it becomes automatic.

Compared to Nothing

I can generally identify citizens who have not been trained in decision-making by how they evaluate the job performance of a president. It is common for citizens to say a president is doing either a great job or a poor job. But . . . compared to whom???

There is no controlled experiment in which the actual president is compared to some other president who is doing the same job, under the same conditions, at the same time. And without that comparison, you can't really tell how much impact the president is having. Would some other president have done better? There is no way to know. If you don't know how any other president would have performed under the same circumstances, you don't really know anything about the president's performance. You couldn't tell the difference between great and poor performance. But you probably think you can.

In 2017, the press and the public were debating whether President Trump did a good job or a poor job in handling Puerto Rico's emergency recovery from Hurricane Maria. You see strong opinions on both sides of that question, which is typical in politics. What was less typical in this situation was that both sides were totally irrational. And they didn't know it.

Here's why.

People who have been trained in decision-making understand that you can't evaluate things in isolation. The only way to know how well President Trump handled the hurricane in Puerto Rico is to compare it to how the other people who were president at the same time in a parallel world handled their Puerto Rico hurricanes, with all variables the same except the president. Obviously that comparison can't be made because we had only one president and one Hurricane Maria striking Puerto Rico in 2017, and that was after two major hurricanes had already stretched FEMA's emergency resources just weeks earlier. There is no rational way to know if the Trump administration did a great job or a poor job. You can only describe what happened, and even that probably lacks complete context. Anticipating your objections to this point, I agree that if Trump acted in ways that were obviously crazy and unproductive, we would know for sure he was doing it wrong. But within the scope of normal(ish) behavior, you can't know for sure that some other president would have performed better.

For example, you can note that pallets of water were never

delivered to people who needed water. But you can't know if another president would have done something differently to cause that water to be delivered. And if that hypothetical other president did a good job of water delivery, would he or she also have done a good job on every other variable? That is unknowable. And that means we can never be sure how well the president performed compared to how well some other president might have performed in the same situation.

That said, I do think you can often identify when a leader is using the right set of tools for the job. For example, you can tell if the leader is using good persuasion technique. But you can never know for sure if some other president might have had the same skills and got an even better outcome.

DILBERT   **BY SCOTT ADAMS**

People also make the mistake of not comparing proposed plans to the next best alternative. Sometimes the best plan has big problems, but not as big as the next best plan. If you are not explicitly comparing your preferred plan to the next best alternative, you are not involved in rational thinking. But it might feel as if you are.

> If you have a strong opinion about a proposed plan but you have not compared it to the next best alternative, you are not part of a rational conversation.

HALFPINIONS

One of the most common decision-making errors you see in politics involves ignoring either the costs or the benefits of major decisions. This might include supporting an idea that would be terrific if it were free, but is in fact something taxpayers would never support. This decision-making flaw is not limited to one side of the political divide. Both sides routinely focus on costs alone or benefits alone, depending on the topic. Rarely do you see politicians or political pundits describe the costs and the benefits of a proposal, at least not in any useful detail. I assume they believe that leaving out half of the decision is more persuasive. And maybe it is when they are preaching to the converted. But if you want to convince people on the other team to change their opinions, it helps to compare the full costs of a plan to the full benefits. Otherwise, you will not be seen as a credible voice, and people who lack credibility rarely change minds.

I call the act of ignoring one half of a topic (either the costs or the benefits) a *halfpinion*.

> If your opinion considers only the benefits or only the costs of a plan, you might be in a mental prison.

TIME VALUE OF MONEY

Our ability to predict what path is the right one depends on looking at both the short-term and the long-term implications of our decisions. As obvious as that point is, the public rarely considers all the costs and all the benefits in discussions about major topics, such as politics.

You'll often see political debates in which one side acts as if today is all that matters and the other acts as if the future is all that matters. Neither is a rational position. If you haven't considered both the now and the later, or you refuse to acknowledge one or the other when you are debating the topic, you are not part of a productive debate.

I sometimes refer to those who focus on the near term as having a child's view of the world. For example:

CHILD: I want candy.

PARENT: Dinner is in a few minutes. It's better in the long run to eat healthy foods and avoid junk food and snacks.

CHILD: But . . . I want candy. Now.

The adult view is that the costs in the near term might be unpleasant, but we will come out ahead in the long term. A rational person considers all the costs and all the benefits of any plan. And those costs and benefits are also compared to alternative plans so you can see which one is best.

In political discussions, you rarely see anything like a full description of the costs and benefits. Political advocates focus on the costs of a plan when they hate it and the benefits when they like it. People who follow politics mimic the advocates and end up with halfpinions instead of full opinions.

Ideally, you want to consider all the impacts of your decisions, both now and later. But the present has one quality that the future does not: certainty. You can often predict with confidence what will happen tomorrow, but predicting events more than a year in the future gets iffy fast. In the business world, no one takes too seriously predictions that are more than three years out. That's a good rule of thumb. Financial predictions that are more than three years out are about as useful as underpants on a robot.

In business terms, you should mentally "discount" any money you expect to receive in the future because a dollar you receive later is worth less than a dollar you receive today. Intuitively, you know you would rather get a dollar today than wait a year for that same dollar. If you wait, something might come up that makes that dollar unavailable to you. And if you have that dollar today, you can use it today, for spending or investing. When it comes to money, sooner is better.

A useful rule of thumb for doing quick mental calculations is that money doubles in value every ten years, assuming you can earn an average 7 percent return per year. A diversified stock portfolio, such as an index fund, could be expected to have at least a 7 percent average return over any multidecade period. Here's what $1 trillion looks like if you invest it instead of spending it all today.

0 years—$1 trillion

10 years—$2 trillion

20 years—$4 trillion

30 years—$8 trillion

40 years—$16 trillion

50 years—$32 trillion

60 years—$64 trillion

70 years—$128 trillion

80 years—$256 trillion

Understanding that a dollar today is worth far more than a dollar in the future, would you spend $1 trillion today addressing, let's say, climate change, to avoid losing $10 trillion in GDP over the next eighty years? If you don't understand the concept of discounting the value of future money, you might think it's a good deal to spend $1 trillion to save $10 trillion. But if you understand that money received in the future is worth less than money received today, you would probably ask how the $10 trillion savings is distributed over the eighty years. If most of the financial benefit comes in early years, you might have a good deal. But if most if it comes toward the end of the eighty years, you'll have to do some calculations to see whether or not that future savings is worth $1 trillion today.

A dollar you have today is worth a dollar. But a dollar you might get in the future, if things go as predicted (which is rare), is worth a lot less.

In the business world, a project that doesn't pay for itself in two to three years is generally a bad idea. The exception is when real estate is involved, because real estate rarely decreases in value over time unless something unusual happens. If you build a factory, the building and land will probably be worth something in ten years even if your underlying business goes bust.

CONSIDER THE ALTERNATIVES

Keeping with the theme of climate change, the risk of climate change isn't only about money, according to the majority of scientists working in the field. The risk is that too much warming could make large parts of the planet uninhabitable. In that case, wouldn't you spend $1 trillion today just in case it is the only way to save the future world? That is the argument you will hear most often about climate risks. If there is even a small chance we are heading toward a near-extinction event, shouldn't we put maximum effort and expense into driving that risk to zero?

Answer: It depends what else you need the money for.

If climate change were the only risk in our dangerous world, then yes, it would be rational to spend—and even overspend—to bring the risk of human extinction to zero. But we live in a dangerous world, with lots of mortal risks. Would we be better off putting that $1 trillion into an asteroid early-warning system, complete with nuclear missiles that could move the asteroids off course if we detect them early enough? What about the risks of pandemics, economic catastrophes, cyberwars, nuclear war, and a dozen other things that could destroy life on earth? On a risk-reward basis, would we be better off using our money to boost the economy now so fewer people die from poverty in the future?

Our financial and technical ability to address climate change will be far greater in ten years than it is now, and we will be far better informed about the true risks and costs of a warming climate by then. Given that situation, would you spend all of your money trying to fix the climate now, or would you keep developing better climate-fixing technologies and growing the economy so we will have more options for addressing climate risks in ten years?

As I often say, humans don't use facts and reasons to make decisions on complicated topics. The opinions of average voters on how to address climate change are driven by fear, emotion, team play, and other irrational factors. We're not capable of sorting out the risks and the economics of complicated events playing out over decades. And given the limits of our resources, we can't spend infinite money to lower every extinction risk to zero. We have to choose our targets wisely, which is a problem, because we do not have a wise public or a wise government.

If you have only one mortal risk, it might make sense to spend huge amounts of money to drive that risk to zero. But if you have multiple mortal risks, it might make more sense to allocate your money across several risks.

CONFUSOPOLIES

Years ago, I coined the word confusopoly to describe an industry in which price competition is eliminated by making products and services so confusing that customers can't tell what they are getting for their money. The best examples are insurance products and mobile phone service. Most consumers can't tell which companies offer the best deals because they can't sort through the complexity. If you do an Internet search on "confusopoly," you will find it referenced by economists around the world. It even has its own Wikipedia page.

Consider the complicated terms of service agreements we encounter nearly every day. That is just the surface. A company such as Nest is a hub for lots of different smart devices, and each company has its own privacy policies. Shoshana Zuboff, author of The Age of Surveillance Capitalism, tells us that a Nest owner would need to review a minimum of one thousand different privacy contracts to make sure there were no unwelcome issues from any of the products that work with your Nest.[1]

The world in general is becoming more of a confusopoly. If you have a firm opinion about international trade deals, the future of cryptocurrencies, or any of a thousand other complicated topics, you might be engaging in loserthink. I say that because no one should be confident in the face of complexity.

You might have arrived at your certainty by trusting experts. But experts can't penetrate complexity either. At least not so often that you can trust the next one to get it right because the last one did. Experts have been wrong—at least some of them have—about nearly every complicated event in history.

To be fair, at least one expert usually gets it right no matter the topic. But how do you know ahead of time which expert will be right? That would require you to be an expert about those particular experts, and you probably are not anything like that.

If you find yourself experiencing certainty in a complex situation, you are probably experiencing loserthink.

STRAIGHT-LINE PREDICTIONS

Economists spend a lot of time trying to predict what will happen to people's money if one or more variables in the world are tweaked. If you try to predict the future by assuming no variables ever change, you get predictions that look like these:

"The horse is here to stay but the automobile is only a novelty—a fad."
—The president of Michigan Savings Bank
advising Henry Ford's lawyer not to invest
in Ford Motor Co., 1903[2]

"The world potential market for copying machines is 5,000 at most."
—IBM, to the eventual founders of Xerox,
saying the photocopier had no market large
enough to justify production, 1959[3]

"There is no reason anyone would want a computer in their home."
—Ken Olsen, president, chairman, and founder
of Digital Equipment Corp., 1977[4]

"Stocks have reached what looks like a permanently high plateau."
—Irving Fisher, professor of economics,
Yale University, 1929[5]

"We don't like their sound, and guitar music is on the way out."
—Decca Records, rejecting the Beatles, 1962[6]

A terrible way to predict the future is to assume things will keep going the way they have been going. The terrible way is also the most common way. And that makes sense because the alternative is predicting "surprises" along the way, and that would be absurd. If we could predict surprises, they wouldn't be surprises.

But predict we must, because that's how we decide how to act. For example, I just made a forty-year projection of my finances to see how much I can spend now and still retire comfortably. And in that forty-year prediction, I didn't account for any social or technological change of consequence. I didn't take into account this book becoming an enormous bestseller. I didn't account for robots, health changes, medical breakthroughs, wars, depressions, alien encounters, climate change, the fate of my startup, the third Adams presidency, or any of a thousand variables that will make my future completely unpredictable.

And those are the big potential changes, or at least a sample of them. My financial future is also entirely different if I tweak my expected investment return by one half of 1 percent. The difference is so large when compounded over forty years that I would act differently today based on using the lower number versus the higher one.

Straight-line predictions told us the population would increase faster than the food supply. The opposite happened. Straight-line predictions told us we would run out of fossil fuels, but we keep finding new sources. We humans are not good at predicting. And any notion that we have developed that superpower, in light of all observations to the contrary, is pure loserthink.

Straight-line predictions are generally wrong, and dangerous if you act on them. Still, they are not useless. Sometimes a straight-line prediction can encourage people to make the changes necessary to avoid a bad outcome. And sometimes you can rule out some possible outcomes, which can be helpful. But don't confuse *helpful* with *accurate*.

When trying to predict the future, I often look to what I call the Adams Law of Slow-Moving Disasters. The idea is that whenever we humans see a huge problem coming at us in slow motion, the odds are excellent that we will figure out a solution. That's why we haven't run out of food or fossil fuels, and why the Y2K bug was solved somewhat easily. So long as we have lots of warning, humans are astonishingly clever at solving problems, even enormous ones. So figure that into your predictions.

I also like to look at how much entrepreneurial energy is going into a topic. For example, in the dawn of the personal computer age, it was hard to know which companies would come to dominate the industry, but it wasn't hard at all to know that personal computers were here to stay. Similarly, we observe there is a lot of energy going into blockchain technologies, which doesn't tell you much about the future of any particular product or company, but we can safely predict that blockchain will be around for a while. In general, when you see a lot of energy in a particular area, spread across multiple companies, the technology or industry is likely to stay around even if the players change. That is helpful to understand when predicting a future that doesn't travel in straight lines.

Over the long term, straight-line predictions are loserthink, because history rarely travels in a straight line.

CHAPTER 11

Things Pundits Say That You Should Not Copy

One of the ways we accidentally build mental prisons for ourselves is by mimicking the irrational arguments we hear from pundits. Pundits are almost always advocates, as opposed to objective observers. If you imitate their arguments, you are leaving the field of reason in favor of trying to persuade. If you are intentionally copying pundits for the purpose of persuasion, that might make sense. But if you are imitating pundits while imagining their opinions are unbiased and rational, you are creating a little mental prison for yourself.

In this chapter, I will show you how to avoid copying the most ridiculous pundit "reasoning," as well as how to avoid falling into their word traps.

MORAL EQUIVALENCY

If you have no children, but you do have a cat, I recommend that you resist the urge to speak as though kids and cats were similar in importance, even if you believe that to be the case. Don't do something like this:

FRIEND: "My kids are driving me crazy with their picky eating."

YOU: "I know what you mean. My cat only eats wet cat food."

That comes off sounding as if you think your cat and your friend's kids are equivalent in some meaningful way. And they are. But you can't say that without making your friend feel bad. So don't do it. Here is another example to avoid.

FRIEND: "I'm having a quadruple bypass tomorrow. The doctor urged me to update my will."

YOU: "I know the feeling. I had a Botox shot to get rid of some wrinkles in my forehead and it was super scary."

As a matter of good manners, try to resist comparing someone's cancer with your pimple, or comparing a death in someone else's family to an expired carton of milk in your fridge. It isn't a crime against humanity; it just isn't good manners. And it is rarely persuasive.

If you are defending your side of an issue by claiming your critics are making a "moral equivalence," you are likely engaging in empty-calorie loserthink. We don't know how people are ranking things unless they tell us explicitly, and then we still suspect they might be lying.

I have yet to see anyone accused of making a "moral equivalence" confirm that they are intending to do so. And that means the typical accusation of "making a moral equivalence" is based on some sort of assumption about what a stranger is thinking. We humans are not good at reading minds, but we often think we have that magical power.

I most often see the accusation of moral equivalence when people can't defend their side but need to say something smart-sounding. For example, if you insult someone at a bar, and a drunk kills you over it, those two acts are not morally equivalent. Murder is generally considered worse than insults. But it is nonetheless true that both parties acted poorly—one more poorly than the other. In a scientific sense, you can blame both participants for their parts in it. But in a political or social media sense, any statement saying both parties are to blame opens you to the loserthink criticism that you are "making a moral equivalence," which is probably not what you are doing.

As a general rule, when people intend to make a moral equivalence, they are happy to confirm they are doing so if you ask for clarification. But if the only people talking about moral equivalence are the pundits, and the target of those pundits is not thinking in those terms at all, the pundits might be lost in loserthink. Don't be like them.

If you are accusing someone of making inappropriate moral equivalences, you are probably experiencing loserthink of the mind reader variety.

WORD-THINKING

When you criticize something that has gone wrong, as all of us sometimes do, you might have a perfectly valid point, especially if you are using facts and logic.

But if you find yourself reengineering the meaning of common words to make your case, you might be engaging in what I call word-thinking, a common form of loserthink. Word-thinking involves trying to understand the world, or trying to win a debate, by concentrating on the definition of words.

EXAMPLE:

PRO-LIFER: Abortion is murder!

PRO-CHOICER: It's only "murder" when it is illegal. And it isn't illegal.

PRO-LIFER: Call it what you will, but killing an innocent human life is immoral!

PRO-CHOICER: A fetus isn't "life" until it can live on its own.

PRO-LIFER: Life begins at conception!

And so on.

You can see in this example that no real debate is happening at all. It is little more than a debate about the definition of words. The real debate involves finding a political balance between one side's preferred sense of morality and the other side's preference for allowing women the freedom to choose their best personal health, lifestyle, and economic outcomes. If you make an honest argument either for or against abortion, you end up looking like a monster, albeit a different kind of monster depending on which side you take. So most people quite reasonably retreat to the safest space on the topic, which is to insist their personal definition of words should determine national laws.

Rarely, if ever, does anyone use word-thinking when the facts and the logic are on their side and they feel safe to discuss them. We generally like to lead with our strongest arguments, and that means you leave the word-thinking as your last resort. In fact, that's one of the ways I know I have won a debate on Twitter. When the word-thinking comes out, I declare victory and walk away.

Let's look at some examples of word-thinking.

"Normalizing"

In political discussions you often hear people saying it would be bad to "normalize" one sort of behavior or another. The implication is that the behavior in question is both abnormal and undesirable. But "normalize" is a vague and subjective standard. What is the difference between normalizing something and simply doing something you think makes sense? How long does a new thing have to last before we call it normalized?

We will never agree on what normalizing means, or even if it's a bad thing or a good thing in any particular situation. For example, you wouldn't want to "normalize" a sitting president criticizing the legitimacy of the press, because press freedom is a core value. But that's making you think past the sale. The first question that must be answered is whether or not the press has crossed a line from legitimate reporting to what some would call fake news that is pushing political agendas on both the left and the right. If that line has been crossed, it seems to me entirely legitimate, as well as productive, for leaders to point it out. On the other hand, if the line has *not* been crossed, we wouldn't want to make it a habit to act as if it had. The word *normalize* in this context influences you to uncritically accept that the press is beyond criticism. That is an example of word-thinking, in which the word *normalize* is used as a substitute for reasons. Words are not reasons by themselves. But they can feel like it.

When people have good arguments, they will more often than not gleefully show their work to anyone who will listen. But when people have no compelling arguments for their points of view, they sometimes prefer to jump ahead to the "Don't normalize that behavior" stage and act like the argument makes itself.

> If your only complaint about another person's behavior is that it might normalize something, you might not have any reasons to back your opinion.

"Problematic"

If you don't like someone's plan, but you don't have specific objections, you might be tempted to label the plan *problematic*. That generic label excuses you from having to provide facts and reasons to back up your opinion. Best of all, the word *problematic* sounds smart, which gives you unearned credibility.

If you tried to describe what you meant by *problematic*, you might sound like this: "I don't see any specific problems with your plan, but I feel as if there must be some." You would be ignored or mocked for having such an empty opinion. But if you say the plan is problematic, you have suggested there is some sort of commonsense reason to expect problems, and geniuses such as yourself can recognize those problems.

To be clear, you might be absolutely right about the risk of unspecified future problems. Some plans are so bad it would take all day to list all the ways they can go wrong. Those situations are indeed problematic. But in those cases, you can probably describe realistic scenarios for how things might go wrong. If the best you can do is label something problematic without offering some reasonable-sounding speculation on exactly how that might be the case, you are engaging in loserthink.

As I said, people who have logic and facts on their side tend to show their work. People who don't have good arguments try to get away with labeling the situation as if the unstated argument were simply obvious.

Consider the topic of freedom of speech. No matter how much you like the right to free speech, you have to agree it can cause some problems. But you can easily list examples of potential problems. For example, you might say bad people will spread damaging ideas. You might say people will lie in public and ruin the reputation of honorable people. If you can point out some reasonable potential problems, it is fair to summarize all of that as problematic. But if you find yourself calling a plan problematic and you can't give some reasonable-sounding examples to back it up, that is loserthink.

If you find yourself calling a plan problematic and you can't give some reasonable-sounding examples to back up your opinion, you might be engaging in loserthink.

THE HYPOCRISY DEFENSE

If you defend your point of view by saying some version of "The other side does it too," you are abandoning the adult frame and entering a child frame. Children say, "My sister did it too!!!" Adults say, "I made a mistake. This sort of mistake is too common. Here's what I plan to do about it."

Refusing to admit your errors, or your team's errors, locks you into a team sport mentality. That's a mental prison. It makes you appear small and it doesn't advance anyone's interests. You're more focused on the fight than the fix.

To escape that mental prison, admit you are wrong, put it in context, and explain what you plan to do to fix it. Then you're free. If your best response to a credible accusation against your team is that the other side does it too, you are locked in loserthink.

> If you make a mistake and your best response is that other people do similar things, you are engaging in loserthink.

FAIRNESS

Humans apparently evolved to prefer fairness in situations where they don't have the option of being on top. And that's most situations. But as a practical matter, fairness is an impossible standard, because it is always a matter of opinion. The closest we can come to fairness involves applying the law equally to all citizens. Fairness beyond that is generally out of reach because what looks fair to me might not look so fair to you.

For example, let's say you're tall and I'm rich. Is that fair? And if it isn't fair, should we try to fix it? Life is like this in the sense that you can rarely measure what is fair and what is not. And if you could measure it, people still wouldn't agree on what they were seeing or what needed to be measured.

You often hear political leaders argue for fairness. Their job is to persuade, so that makes sense. Politicians are advocates for their constituents, not referees for fairness. If your job is to persuade, arguing for fairness can be an effective approach because humans are spring-loaded to prefer fairness. But in everyday life, fairness is an illusion, and complaining about the lack of fairness is rarely productive.

If fairness is an illusion, you might wonder how people can be leaders in a world in which there is no standard for how things should end up. As a practical matter, things usually end up wherever there is the least complaining. That's as close as we can get to "fair." And sometimes the only way to get to that stable state is through persuasion, as opposed to facts and reason.

> Arguing for fairness is loserthink because no two people will agree on what it looks like. The exception is when you are trying to persuade, in which case rationality matters less.

If you find yourself in a debate with someone who is using fairness as an argument, try taking the high ground by saying some version of this: "Fairness is a child's argument. It isn't a useful standard because reasonable adults will disagree on what is fair. The best you can do is play by the same rules."

FEELS-THE-SAME

A good use of an analogy would be, for example, Otto von Bismarck's famous quote that laws and sausages are two things people shouldn't see being made. That does a good job of conveying the point that making laws is an ugly business and the public would lose their faith in government if they could observe the lawmaking process. In this context, Bismarck is just explaining a new idea to us in a memorable way. That is a good use of analogy.

A bad use of an analogy involves saying your neighbor's cat has markings on its snout that look like a Hitler mustache so maybe someone should put the cat to sleep before it tries to invade Poland. If that example sounds ridiculous, consider a meme I saw on Twitter while writing this chapter. Above a photo of President Trump, the meme asked, "Do you know who else discredited the media?" Below the photo came the answer: "Lenin, Stalin, Hitler, Mussolini, Castro, Mao, Idi Amin, Pol Pot, Hussein, Assad, Putin, ISIS, Boko Haram." That meme is based on situations that *feel* similar in at least one way, but that doesn't mean anything else about those characters is similar. Plenty of politicians criticize the media, but few of them become dictators. And frankly, I think most of you would prefer your leaders to criticize the press whenever the press crosses the line from making simple mistakes to naked advocacy.

How you feel about President Trump's criticisms of the press depends on how accurate you think the press has been when covering him. If you believe the press has been willfully inaccurate to the point of delegitimizing itself, any criticism of the press is warranted, even if it comes from a president. If you think the press has been an honest broker of facts, you might believe that criticizing the free press is something only dictators do.

Former president Jimmy Carter, who no one would call a dictator, said this about press coverage of President Trump: "I think the media have been harder on Trump than any other president certainly that I've known about. I think they feel free to claim that Trump is mentally deranged and everything else without hesitation."[1]

As I was writing this book, I noticed a pattern in the eyes of three prominent Democrats: Alexandria Ocasio-Cortez, Cory Booker, and Adam Schiff. I added a fourth image (Charles Manson) on Twitter for humor purposes. Now, I am not saying there is any predictive value to noting that those folks have similar eyes. But you can see how patterns can be persuasive even when they shouldn't be. It's hard to look at those four photos together without reflexively assuming something is wrong with all of them.

Patterns like this one can form mental prisons when they seem to be telling you more than they should. The wide-eyed photos of this group only tell us that four people were photographed on at least one occasion each with their eyes wide open. You can find plenty of photos of these same folks on Google Images with ordinary eye expressions, so

Scott Adams ✓
@ScottAdamsSays

Nothing to worry about here.

all we know is that sometimes their eyes are more open than other times. That is literally all we can know from the photos. But human minds are pattern-recognition machines, and not good ones. We assign meaning to things that are coincidental, or in a case such as this, a manufactured coincidence. I manufactured the coincidence by not showing the majority of photos of each person that are more ordinary in the eye department.

Patterns, and the analogies that often include them, are a form of what I call *feels-the-same*, meaning humans see patterns in lots of things, and those patterns might remind us of other things. But that's all patterns usually mean. If you think an analogy is helping you predict the future, you might be in a mental prison. Analogies don't have that power. To predict the future, look for causation, not patterns.

If you are making near-term predictions based on causation, you might have an accurate view of the world. But if your prediction is based on pattern alone, you are probably in a mental prison. And your jailers are the people who try to dupe you with patterns that mean nothing. I manufactured a meaningless pattern with the bug-eye photos. Your preferred news source intentionally manufactures fake patterns almost every day. Fake patterns add color and interest to boring news stories.

I often say on social media, and elsewhere, that analogies are useless for persuasion. Analogies are also useless for predicting what happens next, especially if the analogies are of the "history repeats" type.

Analogies are great when used for humor. They are also handy for describing a new concept. But I try to avoid using analogies in the service of persuasion or prediction because analogies are not good for that. The target of your persuasion will simply pick it apart for not being exactly the same as the situation you are debating. If you live to be a million, you'll never see anyone win a debate with an analogy.

> **Good use of an analogy (describing something):** His posture reminded me of macaroni.
>
> **Bad use of an analogy (persuasion and prediction):** We should disband the U.S. Postal Service because the Hitler Youth movement started with cool uniforms too. That's where it's all headed.

As bad as analogies are for persuading, they are even worse for predicting. If someone tells you a male lion looks like a gigantic tan-colored house cat with a neck beard, it doesn't help you predict how the lion will work out as a house pet.

If you find that your best argument depends on the predictive or persuasive characteristics of analogies, you are likely in a mental prison of your own making.

FRICTION

In political discussions, you often see partisans talking in binary terms—for example, that a particular plan will completely stop some bad thing, or otherwise it will do nothing. But in the real world, often the best you can do is to create some friction to slow down the things you wish would stop completely.

As I write this page, the United States is debating whether or not border walls (or fences) work. One side says yes and the other says no. Both positions are loserthink. A more productive way to look at the situation is to see that adding friction to anything reduces the number of people who try it. Increasing taxes on cigarettes encourages some (but clearly not all) people to quit. Adding speed traps to highways encourages many people (but clearly not all) to drive closer to the speed limit than they otherwise might. If your goal is zero illegal immigration, walls and fences won't get you there. But if your objective is to substantially reduce illegal immigration, border barriers almost certainly have an impact by adding friction. And you can test how much difference it makes by building a bit of it and measuring how it changes behavior. I guarantee that adding friction changes behavior, in the case of immigration and in everything else in life.

You also see binary thinking around gun control. Critics of gun control will tell you criminals and nuts will still get guns whether they are legal or not, so maybe law-abiding citizens need guns to protect themselves from that crowd. This position ignores the universal truth that friction changes behavior. Gun control certainly wouldn't change the behavior of hardened drug dealers, but a little bit of friction would almost certainly discourage *some* people from stocking up on guns that might someday be used for evil.

Have you noticed that there have been no recent mass shootings in the United States involving fully automatic weapons? It would be reasonable to assume mass shooters prefer the best tool for the job. And yet we observe that they almost always limit their weapon purchases to choices that have less friction both in terms of cost and in raising suspicion via the paperwork. You can buy a fully automatic weapon in the United States, but not without some government-induced friction. If that friction didn't work, surely we would be seeing more mass shootings with fully automatic weapons, because those are the best tools for the evil job. Instead, we see shooters using weapons that can be obtained with the lowest level of friction. In effect, we have already proven that gun control "works" when it introduces friction.

I'm in favor of the Second Amendment, and I realize the issue of gun control is about more than keeping guns from bad people. It is also about freedom, self-defense, sporting, and, for some people, an insurance policy against a government that turns on its people. Those are all important issues. But it is not productive to say gun control "doesn't work" when we observe friction working whenever it is introduced, including with guns.

Adding friction to any human choice will reduce the number of people making that choice. To assume otherwise is loserthink.

MENTIONING IS NOT COMPARING

Let me tell you about some of the things I enjoy in life. I love my girlfriend, good food, exercise, creative ideas, dogs, cats, and world peace. That list seems uncontroversial, doesn't it?

But if someone in a mental prison sees this list, they might write a snarky article or tweet claiming I "compared my girlfriend to a dog."

If you find yourself arguing that someone else has "compared" two things in a way you feel is offensive—but the so-called comparison is in the form of a list—you might be in a mental prison. Sometimes things are on the same list because they have something trivial in common. My grocery list has cheese and fabric softener on it, but that doesn't mean I am comparing cheese to fabric softener. All they have in common is that they come from the same store. One is not being compared to the other.

You might be thinking this "compared to" problem is rare. But if you watch political news, you see it all the time. It's a form of gotcha commentary at worst and of stupidity at best. Let's split the difference and call it loserthink, because it doesn't make anything better for anyone.

If two or more items are mentioned in the same conversation, that doesn't mean anyone is comparing them for relative value.

"DO YOUR OWN RESEARCH"

Pundits and social media trolls like to tell you it is important for you to "do your own research" in order to have informed opinions. Is that rational? Does that make sense?

Sometimes.

In 2004, I lost my ability to speak. My doctors couldn't figure out what the problem was. So I did my own research, using Google, and eventually discovered the name of my condition was spasmodic dysphonia—a fairly rare condition that makes your vocal cords spasm when you try to speak. Once I knew the name of the problem, I sought out experts who treat such things, and they told me it was incurable. I didn't like that answer, so I did my own research and tracked down the only doctor on the planet who was pioneering a new surgical procedure that worked for most but not all patients. After doing some more research on my own, including visiting the doctor, I signed up for the surgery and am now cured.

You might conclude from that story that "doing my own research" works. And I would agree that in the context of healthcare, that's often true. I also think doing your own research helps in areas such as law, construction, and other situations you encounter in your daily life.

The domains in which "do your own research" does not work include anything in the political realm that is big and complicated. In that category I would put climate change, national economic policies, trade negotiations, and gun control. Those are the obvious ones.

In each of those cases, you can research as much as you want, and all you will learn is that there are studies and data supporting opposite positions, and you're not qualified to know which ones are reliable.

For big, complicated political questions, "doing your own research" is a waste of time.

When believers of the Q hoax argued with me on Twitter that Q was a real insider with real predictive powers, they chastised me for not "doing my own research," because that's what they did. At the same time, the nonbelievers in Q were sending the believers long lists of failed Q predictions, easily available with a simple Google search. In this example, which group was "doing their own research"? I'd say both. And did it help them? No. The nonbelievers found evidence that agreed with their beliefs and declared the research complete. The believers pointed to evidence that supported their belief in the Q hoax and declared themselves the best researchers. Both sides declared victory based on "doing their own research."

I'm not against research, of course. And as I said, in many situations, such as your health, doing your own research can be a useful supplement to your normal healthcare. The problem is that "doing your own research" on political topics generally leads people to conclusions that agree with their starting opinions. Confirmation bias looks exactly like knowledge gained from doing your own research. When it comes to political topics, and probably religion too, we humans can't tell the difference between rational opinions and confirmation bias. But we think we can. That's a problem.

Pundits and online debaters often imply they have superior opinions because they have researched a topic more thoroughly. Sometimes those cocky folks are 100 percent right. But other times, they are suffering from confirmation bias, or they are engaged in advocacy instead of reason, and you probably have no way to tell the difference. Doing your own research is usually better than not doing any research, but don't assume you can tell the difference between actual knowledge and your own confirmation bias. There would be no such thing as confirmation bias if we could recognize it when it happened.

"BE YOURSELF"

One of the most dangerous forms of loserthink is the notion that people should "be themselves" or be "authentic"—whatever that means.

This line of thinking imagines your mind is who you are, and there isn't much you can do about it. You were born with a certain personality, either good or bad, and that's the person you will always be. Case closed.

Our DNA does program us to a huge degree. But a more productive way of thinking about your experience in this life is that *you are what you do*. And you have some executive control over what you do. In other words, you can change who you are by changing what you do. For example, learning good manners and making it a habit to use them often will turn you into a polite person even if you weren't "born that way."

One of the best mental habits you can develop is to think in positive terms even when you don't feel positive.[2] For example, I was a negative person in my twenties, but I didn't know it. I thought I was humorously pointing out the flaws in everything around me. I wasn't aware of how damaging it was to the people who had to listen to it. Nor did I realize how the negativity affected my own sense of happiness. Dwelling on the negative is expensive in terms of your social life, your mental health, and even your career success. People like to be around positive people, for all the right reasons.

One day a friend explained to me with brutal honesty (alcohol might have been involved) that I was too negative and it was a drag. I was surprised to hear that my continuous complaining about just about everything wasn't being well received by the people I liked most. So I set out to change that with a simple technique that I borrowed from another friend: if I need to talk about something negative, I pair it with at least one positive thought. I've made such a habit of this over the years that I feel uncomfortable expressing pure criticisms without a healthy dollop of optimism about something—anything—to balance things out.

My original loserthink approach involved complaining any time I was in the mood to do so, under the theory that I was just being me. In my complaining years, I didn't realize I was grinding away on the positive feelings of friends, romantic partners, and coworkers. Now I realize I have a choice not only about how others perceive me but also in creating myself. If I don't want to be a negative person, I simply remind myself to consider the positive in situations as often as I can. Once it becomes habit to do so, that's the person I have become. And I like that person.

> Never be yourself if you can make yourself into something better through your conscious actions. You are what you do.

"COWARD!"

If you're calling someone a coward, you probably aren't saying anything useful. We all weigh the costs and the benefits of decisions before acting. And fear is one of those variables.

After almost any terrorist attack or mass shooting, you will see politicians and pundits proclaim that the perpetrators were "cowards." That is ridiculous. People who sacrifice their lives for causes—including evil causes—are the opposite of cowards. If they were cowards, they wouldn't do what they did.

The problem with labeling terrorists and mass murderers of any kind as cowards, aside from it being ridiculous on the surface, is that it diverts attention from any kind of deeper analysis that would be helpful.

YOU: Why did the killers do it?

PUNDIT: Because they are cowards! Cowards, I say!

YOU: Maybe I'll ask someone else.

It is loserthink to call people cowards after those people risked their lives for a cause.

"APOLOGIST!" AND WORDS LIKE THAT

If you and I agree on a particular issue, you are likely to call me a genius for being on the same side as your nearly divine wisdom. But if we happen to disagree, you might be tempted to label me an "apologist" for whatever badness you imagine I support. No progress can be made when labels substitute for reason.

When your critics have strong arguments, they gleefully offer them. But when those critics have weak arguments, they often try to slap a label on you and hope no one notices the missing reasons. It's a common loserthink strategy. *Apologist* isn't the only word used to sidestep debate. You also see labels such as *narcissist, fascist, globalist, racist,* and *socialist.*

If your intention is to avoid real debate, hurling dismissive labels at your nemesis works great. One has no social obligation to debate with a nemesis that has been labeled into filthy irrelevance. But avoiding debates doesn't move anything forward, it doesn't persuade, and it doesn't make the world a better place.

> If your response to a disagreement is to assign your opponent a dismissive label, you have surrendered the moral and intellectual high ground to wallow in loserthink.

"WHY DIDN'T YOU DO IT SOONER?"

If you have ever held a job or been in a relationship, you know how easy it is for someone to frame your brilliant accomplishments in a way that makes you look lazy and dumb. All it takes is one question: "Why didn't you do it sooner?" There's no good answer to that question, even if you have perfectly good reasons. Your critic will happily tell you that a better and more effective human could have gotten it done sooner, and no one will be able to prove otherwise. It's just your word against the critic, and we are primed by life to believe almost anything could be done faster.

The evil cousin of "Why didn't you do it sooner?" is the question "Why didn't you *tell me* sooner?" Here again, there is no good answer because you always could have called sooner, texted sooner, or done something sooner. There is no such thing as being soon enough. And if you waited, your critic assumes there must be some nefarious reason. Your failure to act sooner is generally seen as hard evidence of your bad character.

If someone does something you are happy about and you praise that person, you encourage more good behavior of the same kind. People like praise and recognition. Most of us are starving for it. Personally, I would probably steal a car if I thought someone would applaud me for it. Praise is an effective way to get more of what you want.

The opposite is also true. When someone does something you appreciate, the best way to ruin that momentum is by asking why it didn't happen sooner. That's putting a penalty on good behavior. And you should expect anyone who gets treated with that sort of loserthink to be less likely to be helpful in the future.

If someone does something you appreciate, it is loserthink to ask why it didn't happen sooner.

I've never discovered a good way to respond to the "Why didn't you do it sooner?" criticism. I can't offer you a solution, but I recommend asking your critics if this is a new standard by which they are also willing to be judged. Do not play defense. Attack the standard for being absurd and unworkable. This approach has zero chance of changing any minds, but you might enjoy asking, "Why didn't you do it sooner?" every time your critic accomplishes something.

This chapter is not an exhaustive list of the ridiculous things pundits and online trolls shamelessly say, but I think it serves as a good reminder that those people are advocates—not logicians, not historians—and they are not always true to the facts. If you choose to imitate their arguments, don't expect others to take you seriously.

CHAPTER 12

The Golden Age Filter

I f you pay attention to the news, you are assaulted with one dire warning after another about how the world is barreling mindlessly toward doom. It is easy to lose sight of the big picture: the world is doing well by historical standards, and the rate of improvement is increasing.

In this chapter, I'll give you a quick tour of what is already going right and what is likely to continue going right. I do this to help you recognize how often you can be in a mental prison of negativity while things are actually going quite well.

I'm an optimist by nature, and I confess to putting that bias on this chapter. But you don't need to buy into all my optimism to see the larger point that you have been sold a negative view of the future because of the business model of the press. If the press has a choice of scaring you or telling you everything is fine, one of those paths is more profitable. Fear sells. I hope this chapter helps you to keep the fear stories in context.

POVERTY AND OVERPOPULATION

In 1966, half of the world lived in extreme poverty. By 2017, the number had fallen to 9 percent.[1] Once you get people out of extreme poverty, they tend to have smaller families, which means you get population control for free.

The middle class has not done so well lately because the cost of living is rising faster than incomes. When an imbalance of this sort happens in an innovative, capitalist system, you can expect new companies to spring up in response. There is always a time lag, of course, so you won't see all of this right away. I'll give you a brief tour of the innovations you can expect in the near future to lower the cost of living.

Inexpensive Homes

We are in the early stages of seeing entirely new home-building systems, but you can already see where things are heading. We're seeing small but successful tests of 3-D-printed homes, factory-built homes, kits for assembling your own home, and nonstandard living arrangements, such as college students being roommates with senior citizens for mutual benefit. It is too early to know which of these approaches will dramatically lower the cost of a good home, but with this much attention on the problem, the smart money says we will soon have low-cost housing options of the type no one can yet fully imagine.

Education

Traditional education involves one instructor teaching a class of students who are in the same room. That's an expensive model, and a bad one if you live in a place with poorly funded schools and no other options. Online learning is rapidly growing and is already cost-effective, but it is fairly primitive compared to where it is likely to evolve in a few years. Most online learning is limited to one teacher droning about a topic while the video camera is running. But eventually, and inevitably, you will see more of a Hollywood film model for online education, meaning teams of qualified people will get together to add their contributions to the product. The "teacher" might simply be a good presenter, similar to an actor. The course content might be the product of graphic artists, CGI artists, gifted writers and directors working together. Now add the tech industry's ability to measure what gets the most clicks and who gets the highest test grades, and you have a way to continuously evolve to better and more effective forms of online teaching.

At the moment, online learning is inferior to a physical classroom experience for most subjects. But that gap will shrink rapidly, and eventually the online experience will be far superior, more widely available, and much less expensive than college. Someday we might see public schools replaced by online courses and augmented by social get-togethers for the students.

I recently bought a virtual reality (VR) system for entertainment and also to learn what is ahead for VR technology. In its current form, the content for VR is limited, and wearing the VR headset for several minutes can give users headaches and motion sickness. But as primitive as the technology is, it is already completely obvious that virtual experiences will eventually rival in-person experiences, and surpass them in many ways. This is especially important for online learning. If you can put yourself into the scene—let's say, attending an historical event as a spectator, or assembling a virtual machine from virtual parts—your learning experience will be extraordinary compared to anything a classroom can provide.

One VR title I used at home involved taking a tour inside the Hindenburg airship that was famously destroyed by a fire in 1937. I could walk through the control room, the crew's quarters, the public spaces, and all the interior engineering spaces at my own pace. This was full-body learning, and I remember the inside of the *Hindenburg* as vividly as if I had been there in person.

Probably the biggest obstacle to nontraditional learning is the value of the degree or certification one gets when done. If you have a degree from a top college, employers know approximately what they are getting. But if you learned a variety of useful skills online, and there is no degree program involved, how would anyone know your value? I expect this to change over time as credible business leaders and companies start endorsing certain collections of online classes as being degree-equivalent.

END OF UNSOLVED CRIME

Have you noticed that nearly 100 percent of high-profile crimes seem to get solved? That's not an accident. In the United States and other developed countries, we have the technology to solve nearly any crime that merits enough resources. You are probably familiar with most of the crime-solving tools available to law enforcement. But when you see them listed together, it creates a powerful picture in which the rate of unsolved crime will approach zero.

Video Everywhere

Most businesses, and an increasing number of private homes, have video security cameras inside and out. If you are running from a crime you've just committed, all law enforcement needs to know is where the crime happened and approximately when, and they can usually find video of you leaving the scene.

I assume most self-driving cars of the future will have video capabilities both inside and out, meaning anything within sight of an automobile is likely to be recorded. And self-driving cars will reduce drunk driving, speeding, road rage, and most other types of vehicle-related crimes.

With the ubiquity of smartphones, you can almost guarantee that any crime in a public space will be recorded. And if the perpetrator makes the mistake of talking anywhere near a smartphone or home speaker, law enforcement might be able to find that audio file.

Digital Trail

If you own a smartphone—and nearly all criminals do—law enforcement can know where you have been, what you have been saying, with whom you have been communicating, and where you purchased what kind of goods. Unless you live off the digital grid, which is rare, you're likely to leave a clear trail.

DNA

We have long been able to match DNA with evidence found at crime scenes. But this capability is taking a huge leap forward as more people voluntarily submit DNA samples for personal testing and for tracing their family trees on genealogical websites.[2] What's new is that a perpetrator's DNA can now be used to locate a cousin or other relative. And once you have a family member, you can usually find the perp. Just ask cousin Bob if he has any relatives living in the town where a crime has happened. That's often enough information to find the criminal, and this exact process has already been successfully used. As more people voluntarily submit their DNA for various personal reasons, any DNA from a crime scene is likely to lead to identification of the criminal via family connections. And once you have a suspect, that person's digital trail will give them away.

Humans will always be tempted to commit crimes, but it usually only happens when people feel they can get away with it. The days of getting away with crime are almost over. Expect crime rates to continue falling.

WORLD PEACE

Experts disagree on whether we are experiencing a trend of declining war in recent decades.[3] Like most things, it depends how you measure it. And comparisons of war dead over time are complicated by improvements in treating the wounded. But in my opinion, a number of forces are aligning to make wars far less likely in the future.

1. Mutually assured destruction keeps working.
2. Conquest is no longer economical.
3. Guerrilla resisters have access to better weaponry.
4. Economic war is a better substitute for physical war.

In olden times, it often made sense to conquer a neighboring country to plunder their resources. It could be a good investment. Today, there is little opportunity for making money from war because the conquered country would inevitably produce a well-armed guerrilla resistance to destroy pipelines, roads, and other economic assets of the conquerors. And we know the aggressor country will suffer staggering economic pressure from the rest of the developed world. In our increasingly connected global economy, making war is bad for business, and the aggressor can know with certainty they will not come out ahead.

If countries will no longer start wars for economic gain, you still have the kinds of wars in which an irrational leader brainwashes his own citizens to fight for irrational reasons. But even the most irrational leaders need to believe they have a chance of winning before they commit to battle. Hitler was crazy, but he invaded other countries only when he thought he had a good chance of winning, both militarily and economically. And in those days, when resistance forces were armed mostly with rifles, you had a good chance of occupying and holding conquered territory. None of that is true in today's world. Conquering your neighbor in this day and age is economic suicide.

If you look at the two alleged "craziest" leaders in today's world who also have substantial militaries—Iran's Ali Khamenei and North Korea's Kim Jong-un—we observe both of them responding rationally to economic pressure and military threats. Keep in mind that the press routinely describes our international adversaries as unhinged, which is almost always an exaggeration. When dictators do evil things to their critics and adversaries, it is generally in a rational, albeit immoral, pursuit of self-interest. In other words, even "crazy" dictators are not full-on crazy.

Given human nature, a dictator who crosses the line into full-on irrationality would soon be removed by his own inner circle and military. While the odds of dictators being labeled crazy by adversaries are 100 percent, the odds of a completely irrational leader staying in power long enough to wage war seems vanishingly small in this day and age.

I'll round out my optimism about the direction of war by looking at some of the main types of military conflicts.

Nuclear Powers

We have never seen two nuclear powers go to war against each other, and in my opinion we never will. The threat of mutually assured destruction is clearly effective. The minimum requirement for starting a war is that the aggressor has to think there is a legitimate chance of winning, and no one believes a country can win a nuclear war in any sense that "winning" means something. So that's good news.

Nuclear Powers Attacking Nonnuclear Powers

The lesson of the past few decades is that large military powers can easily crush countries with smaller militaries. But the victor can't easily occupy and hold the defeated country for the long run because of the high cost of containing the inevitable guerrilla resistance. So we will probably see fewer wars of conquest simply because they don't work out for the conquering power.

Proxy Wars

Big countries like to take sides in wars fought by small countries, including revolutions, whenever it suits the larger country's national interest. We call those proxy wars. For the larger countries supporting fighters in smaller countries, the benefits of having your side prevail can outweigh the risks. Or at least that has been the case in the past. But here too we see a trend toward economic punishment of the larger countries backing a warring faction. For example, at this writing, both Iran and Saudi Arabia are experiencing economic pressure to end their proxy war in Yemen.[4]

Special-Case Wars

We will still see smaller wars for years to come in which there is some kind of special case involved. For example, if a conquered country's citizens are neutral or positive about the conquering country's intentions, and they dislike their own leaders, that situation might be economical for the conquerors. But over time, we should expect the number of special cases to shrink toward zero as those few situations are exploited.

Radical Islamic Wars

I see no end in sight for radical Islamic terror attacks because the normal cost-benefit analysis of life on earth doesn't apply to people who believe their payoff comes after martyrdom. But the brief tenure of the so-called ISIS caliphate in Syria shows us what happens when overachieving terrorists try to hold territory: it turns them into easier targets. The advantages of being a secret terror society evaporate when you try to hold territory.

We also observe that the psychological situation in the Middle East is evolving in a positive way. The old thinking was that Israel was the common enemy of its Muslim neighbors and susceptible to some kind of eventual conquest. The newer thinking is that Israel is too strong to conquer in any rational military sense, and Iran is emerging as the common enemy of both Israel and other Muslim countries in the region. Israel has made tremendous progress in improving relations with its neighbors and has made a public campaign of friendship directly to the Iranian people, offering to help them with water purification, for example.

Put all of this together and the Middle East might be only one ayatollah away from something that looks like peace. And that ayatollah, Iran's Supreme Leader Khamenei, is in his eighties, with a crumbling economy thanks to sanctions and military spending, and a relatively pro-Western population. For perhaps the first time ever, conditions are ripe for major progress in eliminating war in the Middle East.

Miscellaneous Wars

Afghanistan will probably be at war with itself, with the help of various outside entities, for another hundred years. But most of that will stay within its borders. And it is reasonable to assume plenty of underdeveloped countries will have civil wars and wars with neighbors, complete with genocides and atrocities. But as countries in that category develop their economies and become tied into the global economic system, their odds of war will plummet.

For the developed world, as well as their less-developed allies, the risk of war is declining every year because economic sanctions are the better weapons of choice.

I won't argue with anyone who tells me I am too optimistic about the future of major wars. But I am certain that the historical reasons for war have nearly evaporated, at least in terms of the largest military powers. Today, economic war makes far more sense, and I don't see that changing.

CLIMATE CHANGE

In 2018, the Intergovernmental Panel on Climate Change (IPCC) released a "dire" prediction that climate change could depress GDP by 10 percent in eighty years. That might be the best news you have heard on the topic, albeit disguised as terrible news. In eighty years, the world is likely to be five to ten times wealthier, assuming normal trends, and we wouldn't even notice we were 10 percent worse off than we might have been without climate change.

But let's say you don't believe global warming is economically trivial. You still have reason for optimism because of the technologies that are already in the pipeline. And one can hardly imagine what we will see over the next eighty years. Here are some interesting developments in that space.

Fusion Power

Fusion power has been the "flying car" of energy conversations for many years. Futurists have consistently predicted it is coming soonish, only to leave us disappointed as the future comes and goes without it.

The dream is that fusion will be the nuclear technology that overcomes a number of limitations with older fission technology. The potential of fusion power, should it ever be solved to a commercial level, is immense. Fusion would provide clean, uninterrupted power at a cost that would annihilate all competing sources. If scientists and engineers can commercialize that technology in the next twenty years, you can worry a lot less about climate change over the next eighty.

But is fusion ever going to be practical?

Recently I spoke to a brilliant investor in this field who told me the challenges for fusion power have moved out of the realm of science and into the realm of engineering. By that I mean fusion reactors work on paper, and it should work in the real world too, so long as we can engineer a sufficiently powerful set of magnets to contain the plasma, or some other engineering work-around. And there have been big breakthroughs in materials science that should allow us to experiment our way to a stable engineering solution. There are a number of other engineering obstacles, but at this point they all seem to be in the realm of the solvable. At this writing, ten funded startups are pursuing different paths to what they see as the best fusion engineering solution. Would you bet against all ten, knowing they are staffed by some of the smartest people in the world?

Generation IV Nuclear Power

We might not need to wait for fusion technology. So-called Gen IV nuclear reactors are designed so there can be no meltdowns even if nearly everything goes wrong at the same time. Bill Gates called attention to the potential of these "new-wave" reactors in his 2019 list of breakthrough technologies.[5]

Meanwhile, in 2019 the U.S. Department of Energy announced a Versatile Test Reactor site for rapid testing of new nuclear fuel solutions. One of the biggest problems with nuclear power designs is that it is impractical to iterate from poor designs to good designs—the way nearly every other technology evolves—because of the risk, cost, politics, and long planning cycles of anything involving nuclear power. The new rapid-testing facility will address some of that problem.[6]

But what about storing all the nuclear waste from those Gen IV nuclear sites, you ask? Some of the Gen IV designs convert that spent fuel into power.

Anecdotally, I don't know a single smart person who understands the nuclear industry and who also opposes Gen IV nuclear plants. And that includes people who are concerned about climate change and those who are not. Gen IV nuclear seems to be the smart path in either case. And the obstacles to it are falling away quickly.

Air-conditioning

One of the bigger risks of climate warming is that more people will die from heat. Billionaire entrepreneur Richard Branson has teamed up with the Indian government to offer a $3 million prize to whoever can invent a better air-conditioning system—meaning a less expensive one. This sort of concentrated effort has produced good outcomes in the past. In a few decades, we might see new forms of low-cost air-conditioning at the same time as cheap electricity from fusion or Gen IV nuclear power. And more generally, eighty years is a long time in which to figure out how to beat the heat. Humans are good at solving problems they can see coming for decades. The smart money says fewer people will be dying from the heat in eighty years, even if temperatures rise as predicted.

CO_2 Scrubbers

Climate change skeptics remind us loudly and often that CO_2 is good for plants, and science agrees. Greenhouses use CO_2 generators to improve plant yields. The big question is how much CO_2 is too much, warming-wise or otherwise. I'm not qualified to address that question, so for our purposes here I will describe some technologies under development for cleaning CO_2 out of the air. I take it as a given that, should we become so good at removing CO_2 from the air that the plants start gasping for it, we will see that problem coming with plenty of time to avoid overshooting the mark. No matter what you believe about the dangers of CO_2, it can't hurt to have technologies that can scrub it out of the air should we feel it is necessary. Here are some things coming our way.

Carbon Engineering

Carbon Engineering is a Canadian company funded in part by Bill Gates. They report having a breakthrough technology for scrubbing CO_2 out of the air and converting it to a type of jet fuel. Their technology already works in a pilot plant, and their big claim is that they have reduced the cost of the process to the point of being economical.

One must be appropriately skeptical of any claims coming from new companies and new technologies. But Bill Gates's involvement suggests the company's ambitions are solidly in the not-so-crazy category.[7]

Climeworks

Climeworks is another company working on scrubbing CO_2 out of the air using giant air-sucking engines and controlled chemical reactions. The company can build these relatively small facilities today, but obviously at a higher cost per unit than if they were implemented on a larger scale. And one assumes the efficiency will improve over time. Adding some cheap nuclear energy to the cost structure would help a lot.[8]

CarbFix

CarbFix is a project run by an international consortium, led by Reykjavik Energy and with funding from the EU. They claim to already be able to scrub CO_2 from the air and store it permanently in rocks. Here again, we must be skeptical about the economics of this sort of thing. But with multiple projects operating to scrub CO_2 out of the air, and an assumption of improved efficiency and lower cost per unit over time, this could be promising.[9]

Global Thermostat

A company named Global Thermostat has developed technology for using the heat generated by existing industrial processes, such as metal smelting, cement production, and petrochemical refining, to collect CO_2 out of the air. The CO_2 can then be used by indoor farms, in oil well rejuvenation, and to make carbonated drinks, for example.

Now imagine using inner-city land that has been cleared of blight and is available at almost no cost because cities own the foreclosed land and want to use it productively. There are tens of thousands of blight-cleared urban properties available across the country. Now imagine you build a data center that generates lots of excess heat and put it next to an indoor farm. Use that excess heat for the indoor farm in the winter, and perhaps also use the heat to warm sidewalks and parking lots so they don't need to be shoveled. Then add the Global Thermostat technology to use the heat from the data center to generate CO_2 for the connected indoor farm. Greenhouses already pipe in CO_2 because it is essential for healthy plant growth.

I won't claim this particular idea is a winner, but it might help you see how unpredictable the future is. Humans have an exceptional track record of solving big problems they can see coming from a long way off. And a "systems approach," in which you design neighborhoods and businesses to work in harmony with each other, has tremendous potential for solving a wide variety of society's problems.[10]

Strata Worldwide

Strata Worldwide also makes a stand-alone commercial product for scrubbing CO_2 out of the air.[11] By now you get the idea. Capitalism is doing its thing.

I'M NOT QUALIFIED to compare any of the CO_2-scrubbing technologies, or to predict which, if any, will be commercially successful. But I liken this situation to the dawn of personal computing. In those days, you couldn't easily predict which companies would come to dominate the market for personal computers, but you could predict with confidence that personal computers were here to stay, and that they would improve dramatically over time. Given the high priority of climate change, and the huge amounts of money that will be funneled in that direction, an optimist such as myself would predict that direct scrubbing of CO_2 from the air will be economical and scalable in time to make a meaningful difference in CO_2 levels on the planet.

In February 2019, Energy Secretary Rick Perry announced $24 million in funding to support eight identified projects in the field of carbon capture. We can't know that any of those projects will succeed, but the energy and attention being applied to carbon capture tells us that plenty of smart people see this as potentially productive.

END OF UNEMPLOYMENT

Most futurists see a world ahead in which robots take all the low-skilled jobs, and even many of the high-skilled jobs, creating massive unemployment. That's one way the future could go, but humans are plucky and adaptable, especially when the problem is so clear and we all agree it's coming. The robot-caused employment crisis is easy to see coming, and I observe some helpful trends that could save us from runaway unemployment.

The first trend is that we are likely to see big innovations that could lower the cost of living. I predict big strides over the next two decades in lowering the cost of healthcare, transportation, energy, education, Internet access, and housing. And that means lower-paying jobs will be sufficient for enjoying a quality life.

I've mentioned that energy costs could drop fast when fusion or

Gen IV nuclear power becomes doable. And the energy industry keeps improving its efficiency in every domain. New homes with efficient solar panels and lots of green construction methods will approach zero-net-energy use, on average, in the coming decades.

Self-driving cars will someday make individual car ownership unnecessary. The cost of owning a vehicle could be spread across multiple families as efficient ride-sharing apps are developed. And self-driving cars will be almost accident-free, which means insurance costs will eventually drop.

Education will continue to move online and improve in effectiveness, and that means the cost of training workers will drop. It will soon be practical and easy to retrain unemployed people.

As I mentioned earlier, I've been looking into low-cost home construction trends, and there is a lot happening in that field. The next five years will see inexpensive homes built by 3-D printers, robots, and even homeowners doing construction themselves using snap-together kits.

Collectively, these trends suggest that a worker who loses a high-paying factory job to robots could have a perfectly good lifestyle on half the income working at a different job. That might require relocating from an expensive location to one that has been developed for low-cost living, but that can be done.

Low-cost living is also critical for senior citizens on fixed incomes. That demographic can't rely on the government to tax its younger citizens enough to give everyone a safety net forever. As an optimist, I expect capitalism to do what it does best: namely, identify a market opportunity and rapidly innovate to create low-cost living options.

The biggest advantage job seekers will have in the future is the ability to find work anywhere in the country—or perhaps in the world—and move there on demand. At the moment, physical mobility is deeply limited for people who have no money. But you can expect normal continuous improvement in that area, just as we see in every other field. Future employers are likely to offer job relocation solutions for low-income people, including better matching of people to jobs, video interviews, inexpensive transportation, and low-cost housing upon arrival. For companies to do otherwise would mean not having access to the best workers.

I also predict a massive job market for renovating existing buildings to make them more energy efficient and more suited for modern living. Robots will soon be able to build new homes by following directions, but they will have a tough time navigating all the decisions that go into a renovation. The renovation market should produce an increasing number of jobs for humans for a long time.

HEALTHCARE INNOVATIONS

The healthcare field is too massive to cover in this sort of book, but we see incredible breakthroughs happening in every area. I'll describe a few trends that promise to lower the cost of healthcare, which addresses one of the biggest problems in the United States.

Telemedicine

My healthcare provider was one of the first to allow patients to do doctor "visits" by email. About 80 percent of the time I get a full solution, including drug prescriptions, within an hour of emailing my doctor. Other healthcare providers are offering similar services. Using email obviously lowers the cost of doctor visits while being more convenient and efficient at the same time.

If email isn't fast enough, or you want a more personal touch, you can now contact a doctor on short notice via a video call on your phone, at a discounted cost to an in-person visit. For people with no healthcare insurance, this is often a big money saver compared to visiting an emergency room for something that isn't an emergency. My startup's app, called Interface by WhenHub,[12] is one of a growing number of platforms for connecting to doctors (and any other kind of expert) by video call. By the time you read this book, I expect the number of tele-medicine options will be far greater.[13]

Smartphone Health Tests and Lab Tests

Devices for testing your health are shrinking in cost and size and be-coming consumer products. Startups are making smartphone accesso-ries that can test your urine, blood, blood pressure, hearth rhythms, temperature, and blood oxygen, to name a few. You can even diagnose your own mole. By the time you read this book, I expect startups will have announced dozens more inexpensive health sensors that work with your phone.

I've invested in startups that use technology recently developed by government military labs to test skin and blood samples on tabletop devices in the doctor's office and give results in minutes. That elimi-nates a lot of the cost of sending samples to labs. Meanwhile, medical lab startups are looking to disrupt the lab-testing business and dramat-ically bring down costs. All indications are that the cost of lab testing—at least for the most common tests—will plummet in coming years.[14]

Innovation and Technology

In 2018, Berkshire Hathaway, Amazon, and J.P. Morgan teamed up to create a better healthcare solution, at a lower cost, for their U.S. employ-ees.[15] That effort is in its early stages, but it looks like it is the right team to innovate and attack some of the toughest cost problems in healthcare. You can expect some or all of the innovations they come up with to eventually benefit the country at large. Amazon's expertise in online selling, data management, and efficient delivery are the obvious places to expect improvement. But I would expect far more from this team. I don't believe a more qualified and well-funded group has ever focused on the problem of healthcare expenses.

MRI Scanners

In the United States, MRI scans are expensive procedures, costing anywhere from a few hundred to a few thousand dollars, depending on the type of scan. Newly developed technologies for making MRI scanners are expected to lower the cost of the devices by half. This is part of a larger trend of startups targeting high-cost medical device markets and building low-cost devices to compete.

Removing Regulatory and Legal Obstacles

The healthcare situation in the United States is burdened by a tangle of rules and regulations that have evolved over time to choke out the benefits of free markets and competition. One assumes that healthcare lobbyists, the natural complexity of the topic, and an inefficient government are the base problem. But there is reason for *some* optimism, as the Trump administration is making a major push to modify federal laws and processes to improve competition in all areas of healthcare. It is too early to know how all that will shake out, but efficient market competition is generally good for consumers.

We might also see some benefits coming from the competition among major political parties in how they propose to address healthcare.

Democrats want some sort of taxpayer-funded universal healthcare while Republicans favor improving market competition to increase access and affordability. From a political perspective, the Democrats have the stronger case because their plan is easy to understand and the average voter isn't concerned that the rich will be overtaxed to pay for it. Here I am intentionally oversimplifying, because that's how voters will see it.

Republicans are in a weaker political position on healthcare because their preferred approach of improving market competition probably sounds to voters like vague promises. And it is hard for Republicans to get credit for changing laws and regulations that voters didn't know were problems in the first place. Still, I expect Republicans to push hard at streamlining regulations and laws to defend against the Democrats' plan for universal healthcare. They need to show concrete results from their policies. Competition is good, even in politics.

Big Data

The more we know about the everyday choices and health details of individuals, the better equipped we will be for understanding which actions improve health and which ones do not. As a country, we already collect massive data from fitness sensors, personal apps, DNA tests, and healthcare records. The usefulness of that sort of data starts small but increases rapidly as you add data. I'll give you a few examples to make the point, but don't put too much stock in the specific examples. I'm making a broader point.

For years I had been taking one baby aspirin every night before bed because doctors said it could help me survive a heart attack. But a recent study found that older people who do not have any special cardiovascular risk get no benefits from the aspirin and, on average, it might slightly increase your risks of other health problems. At the moment, we can only learn this sort of correlation (if not causation) by funding studies. But at some point in the near future, we might have enough patient health data in one database to know whether or not the aspirin takers have longer or shorter life spans, all other things being equal. Broadening the point, the more we know about people's actions and health outcomes, the easier it will be to find out what *combinations of things* are good for you.

As I write this chapter, I am on a working vacation at a site 8,300 feet above sea level. I am told by one of the staff at the hotel that about half of the people who come here will experience flu-like symptoms from the altitude, for a day or two. Wouldn't it be useful to know what makes some people experience those symptoms and some people not? Do we differ in DNA, or in lifestyle, or weight? If I knew I was in the half of the population likely to have bad symptoms (which I did), I could have spent a day in the town halfway down the mountain to acclimate before going higher, which I learned is a common practice here.

My examples might be unimpressive, but the larger point is that with enough data on people's health and actions, we can unlock enormous healthcare value. The potential for saving money by having better patient data is enormous.

Medical Breakthroughs

Medical science has moved forward for centuries, but in recent years the pace of that change is accelerating. We're seeing breakthroughs in gene therapy, stem cell therapy, cancer treatments of all kinds, and vaccine delivery systems, to name a few. Some of our most horrible and expensive medical problems will soon have routine fixes.

If your body were an automobile, we are leaving behind a time in which all you could do for upkeep was to add gas and rotate the tires, and we are entering an age in which we can rebuild every part from scratch. The changes we already know are coming are not incremental in nature. They are game-changers.

The trends I've mentioned above have the collective effect of lowering future healthcare costs dramatically. New healthcare solutions for things we previously couldn't treat will add to healthcare costs, but that trade-off is acceptable for solving previously unsolvable problems.

RACE RELATIONS

If you make the mistake of paying attention to the news, you might think race relations in the United States have deteriorated to an alarming degree. I believe that is mostly an illusion caused by the business model of the press. Bad news sells, and bad news about the Trump administration sells better than anything, according to CNN boss Jeff Zucker. The fire hose of biased news coverage blinds us to any positivity we might otherwise notice.

My favorite example of that was when the press hammered President Trump for what they claimed was his habit of criticizing African-American women. This, they said, was clear evidence of his alleged racism and disrespect for women. The president did criticize several high-profile African-American women within a few weeks, and that was enough to create a pattern in the mind of the president's critics. What they left out of their analysis was that President Trump insults 100 percent of his critics, no matter what demographic group they are in. The very next week he was tweet-slamming several white males, and anyone else who needed it.

My interpretation of this situation was that the reason so many black women were being targeted by the president was because those women were extraordinarily successful in their careers—so much so that the president of the United States had to address their criticisms. The women Trump criticized were playing the blood sport of politics at the very highest level. One of the greatest success stories in race equality you will ever see was widely reported as the opposite. If the president of the United States is attacking you for your criticisms, you're doing a lot right in your career.

The week I was writing this chapter, President Trump tweeted that his fired secretary of state, Rex Tillerson, the former CEO of Exxon, was "dumb as a rock" and "lazy as hell." Old, rich white guys are not safe from the president's counterattacks. The proper context here is that Trump attacks anyone who attacks him first.

Personally, I found it inspiring (and I mean this literally) that so many African-American women had achieved the same target value as Rex Tillerson. A lot of black women in America are experiencing sensationally successful careers, and that is a deeply positive sign.

I live in California, and I won't pretend my experience is typical of the rest of the country. But from my perspective, race relations on a person-to-person level are better than ever. There is more interracial marriage, historically high employment rates for all minority groups, and a generally improved comfort with each other as friends, mates, and neighbors.

If it seems to you there are more racist groups in the country lately, keep in mind that the people who track those things, such as the Southern Poverty Law Center, are paid to find it. If you pay me to track the number of racist groups in the country, I'm not going to skip the three guys in South Dakota with a website they made all by themselves. If you pay someone to find ghosts and eradicate them from your home, the service you hire will probably tell you they found those ghosts. Don't trust data from people who have a financial incentive to find lots of whatever it is you are tracking. And never, ever believe the bad news you hear in the press is as bad as they say when there is a political di-mension to the story, because in those cases the press is generally just taking sides.

If you see an increase in racism in your daily experience, that is a big red flag and you should not ignore it. But if the only place you see an uptick in racism is on the news or as reported by groups paid to find a lot of it, maintain some skepticism. In my opinion, based on living for several decades, racism in America has declined every year of my life. And next year looks good too.

IN SUMMARY . . .

In this chapter, I've tried to frame several global challenges as being not as scary as you originally thought. You can disagree with my opti-mistic opinion in a number of places, and I'm sure you will, but that would still leave enough of my examples to make you wonder why you were worrying as much as you were.

The business model of the press guarantees you will see more negativity than the facts support. Things are often better than they seem, especially in the long run.

As I mentioned earlier, fear is a great motivator, and when humans fear something, they get to work trying to solve the problem. In my optimistic opinion, our current biggest problems are likely to go the same way as our past biggest problems—meaning we'll figure out how to deal with them.

CHAPTER 13

How to Break Out
of Your Mental Prison

I t would be unkind of me to show you the walls of your mental prison without also showing you how to break out. I'm about to share with you the tools and techniques for doing just that. Once you are free of your mental prison, almost every part of your life will get easier, and you will understand the world at a level most people never get to appreciate. You will also be a more effective thinker and more able to contribute to the coming Golden Age.

MY MENTAL PRISON BREAKS

It might help you to know about my own mental prison breaks, so you can get a better feel for what is possible when you free your mind. My mother raised me to believe I "could do anything" so long as I set my mind to it. That was hyperbole, of course, because I can't play the center position for an NBA team. But the mindset of *you can do anything* was a tremendous advantage for me in how I've approached life. I believe no mental prison could hold me, and I've lived my life that way.

I became one of the top cartoonists on the planet without any formal training.

I became one of the highest-paid and most sought-after professional speakers in the country by starting out incompetent and figuring out how to improve.

I became a number-one bestselling author with my first book, The Dilbert Principle. This book will be my eleventh, not counting dozens of Dilbert books. I have never taken a writing class, unless you count a two-day workshop on business writing.

A few years into my cartooning career, I acquired an incurable muscle spasm with my drawing hand called focal dystonia. The top expert in the country explained to me that it was incurable. It is my understanding that I'm the first known person to find a cure for it. I did that through trial and error plus finding some work-arounds to prevent reinjuring my hand.

As I mentioned earlier in the book, I was born with an "incurable" condition called paruresis, better known as shy bladder. Paruresis is almost impossible to beat, but I'm largely free from it now, having found a way out that works for me.

In 2004, I lost my ability to speak for over three years, thanks to an incurable problem called spasmodic dysphonia. My vocal cords would spasm when I tried to talk. After several years of hunting for a solution, I became one of a few dozen people on the planet to find a cure through what was a new surgical method.

In 2015, I made an unexpected pivot to political commentary, becoming one of the most followed and quoted opinion-makers in the country.

Those are the stories I can tell you. The stuff I can't talk about, for a variety of different reasons, is far more mind-boggling.

You can see from my odd life arc that I don't recognize artificial limits on what I can do or what I can accomplish. I have to wonder what it would have been like if I had been raised to believe there were limits on what I could do. Would I have walked through so many imaginary prison walls in my life, or would I have believed in the existence of those walls and stayed in my mental prison? I don't know. But I do know I have seen plenty of older adults break out of their mental prisons and do great things. So apparently it doesn't matter at what age you plot your escape. You don't need to be raised to ignore your prison walls, as I was. You can start today. And if you are reading this sentence, you are already halfway free.

Let's finish the job.

CULTURAL GRAVITY

Every culture has its own feelings about success. I call that *cultural gravity*. If your culture celebrates success, you have low cultural gravity, and you can rise according to your talents and efforts. But if your culture disapproves of success, you'll feel it dragging you back to earth every time you try to succeed.

When I was in school, I got the highest grades in my class among the boys. Don't be too impressed. It was a small town with only forty people in my entire graduating class, and two of my female classmates had better grades than I did for most of my school life. As you might imagine, the other boys in the class sometimes teased me about being a nerd. That teasing, especially at a young age, created a cultural gravity. The message was clear: if I wanted to be cool, I couldn't also be a good student.

But I was largely immune to the teasing. For every person who tried to put a bad spin on my good grades, ten people were clearly rooting for me to succeed. My small town had low cultural gravity. It was a mostly Republican town, and if you worked hard and followed the rules, you could feel the culture supporting you. The wind was at my back from day one. In the interest of completeness, I have to say it helped a lot to be male. The girls in my school were getting no such support in those backward days. They experienced strong cultural gravity and an unfair expectation that marriage was their career path. The acceptable alternatives were becoming a teacher or a nurse.

We observe what seems to be consistent cultural support for success among the Asian-American communities. In that culture, getting good grades is a cause for celebration and respect. In other words, they have low cultural gravity.

The African-American culture in urban areas apparently has a different situation. That's what I hear from members of that community. Here I do not rely on my own observations. I listen to the people who experienced their own cultural gravity and report on it. I'm told that a young black student in an inner-city area will have a lot of pressure to underperform and to break the rules in order to fit in. I don't have any visibility on why that is the case, but I accept that it is.

As I write this chapter, Kanye West (you might call him Ye) is experiencing some of the most intense cultural gravity you will ever see. He is stepping outside his comfort zone, his brand, and even his experience level to try to improve the country. Anyone with a bit of knowledge about Ye's history knows he has succeeded at the highest levels in both music and fashion, and in both cases he waded into the fields without already being an expert. Evidently, Ye doesn't do loserthink. He is also unusually free of cultural gravity. And for that reason alone, one could argue he is one of the most important public figures on the planet. He isn't just succeeding across multiple fields—he's destroying loserthink and modeling how to escape cultural gravity. Forget about his success in music, his success in fashion, and whatever success he obtains in improving society or politics; Ye is showing the world how to think more productively. That's Gandhi-level stuff, but it might be invisible to those who have feelings about him personally or musically.

> If you allow the opinions of unsuccessful people in your culture to hold you back, you're engaged in loserthink. If you can learn to think of yourself as free from the cultural gravity of your peers, it will pay off in the long run.

KNOWING WHERE TO START

If you don't know the right way to do something, try doing it wrong, so long as it is not dangerous to do so. Doing things wrong is an excellent way to figure out how to do things right. I became one of the most successful cartoonists in the world by doing just about everything wrong until I figured out how to do it right. I became one of the highest-paid speakers at major events by being terrible at it until I understood what worked and what didn't.

When you do something the wrong way, the people who know how to do things the right way will generally jump in to tell you what you are doing wrong. Take advantage of all that free advice.

If you don't know how to do something the right way, and Googling doesn't help, the only alternative to doing things the wrong way is to do nothing at all. That's loserthink. Waiting until you know how to do something exactly right is a poor strategy. You could be waiting forever. Better to jump in, make your mistakes, and see what kind of free assistance that attracts.

In 2016, I started doing livestreaming programs every day on the

Periscope app, talking mostly about persuasion and politics. My content had sketchy audio quality, bad lighting, unfocused topics, and generally the lowest production values you have ever seen. My small audience made continuous suggestions on how to improve all dimensions of my video streams, and I experimented with my own ideas as well. Today, my branded "Coffee with Scott Adams" Periscopes are followed by most of the major news media and have led to book deals and nonstop media requests for interviews. When I'm in public these days, I'm more often recognized for my political commentary than for being the *Dilbert* cartoonist. And I got to this place by being bad at nearly everything until I attracted enough free advice to make progress.

Loserthink involves waiting until you know how to do something right before you do anything at all. That strategy makes sense only when it is physically or financially dangerous to make a mistake. For most ambitions in life, we can jump in, make some mistakes, and figure it out from there. If you get embarrassed in the process, good for you! It means you just learned that embarrassment doesn't kill you. And that, my friends, is like a superpower.

If you can't figure out how to do a task the right way, do it the wrong way and watch how quickly you get free advice.

UNFOCUSED PRIORITIES

One way you can lock yourself in a mental prison is to get your priorities wrong. But getting your priorities right is not as easy as it sounds.

For example, years ago I took the GMAT—the test you take to qualify for U.S. graduate schools in business. The test asked students to read a brief story about a business situation and identify the "most important" variables. I completed several practice tests before taking the real GMAT, and while I got the answers on my practice tests right every time, I noticed that the people who designed the answer sheet did not. In other words, their opinions of what was "most important" differed from mine. I'm still fairly confident my answers were right and the official answers were wrong. In later years, they removed those question types, probably because people like me complained. My point is that it is often deceptively difficult to know what is "most important" in any complicated situation, and even harder to get two people to agree.

Sometimes priorities are clear, such as when there is a risk of physical harm or some immediate emergency. But in our everyday lives, we often can't tell what is most important at any given moment. It's a judgment call, and as I am sure you have noticed, people have bad judgment.

In my book *How to Fail at Almost Everything and Still Win Big*, I talked about making yourself your top priority, because you can't do much for others if you don't first learn how to take care of yourself. That means making your health and your finances your top priorities until those things are in good shape. Then you are in a position to expand your generosity outward, in roughly this order of priority.

PRIORITIES RANKED

1. You
2. Family
3. Friends
4. Employer
5. Town/city
6. Country
7. World

Obviously there are exceptions to this ranking, but you will recognize them when you see them. For example, if you can solve a major problem for the world, please do. We'll all thank you for it, and even your family and friends will appreciate your sacrifice. But that's a rare situation. The more typical situation might be, for example, wondering whether you should work late versus going to the gym. The correct answer is usually the gym. I'll trust you to know when to make an obvious exception.

I recommend being selfish when it comes to your health, fitness, diet, and education. Your job is a high priority too, and you will need to sometimes put your employer first, as that is why they pay you. But if your boss consistently makes you choose work over health, look for a new job.

> Your first priority should be you. If you don't take care of yourself first, you won't be much use to anyone else. But hurry up—the world has lots of problems and maybe you can help.

CONTEXT

Probably the most common way people fall into mental prisons is by not knowing the context of a situation. If you glance at the news headlines on any given day, you'll be surprised how many so-called news stories are nothing but people misunderstanding what someone said or did because some context was missing.

Speaking of missing context, this morning I was doing my daily live Periscope when the mood of the audience suddenly turned. My normally friendly viewers started a chorus of Boo! Boo! Boo! I didn't know what I had done to deserve their disdain. It takes a lot of practice to speak on a live video stream for an hour and also pay attention to live comments coming across the screen. I immediately allocated half of my brain to continuing with my live presentation and the other half to figuring out where I had gone wrong, so I could correct whatever I had said to offend. I soon learned that using half of my brain made me the approximate mental equivalent of an elderly dolphin. I probably could have learned a trick in return for a fish treat, but I wasn't having much luck talking about a complicated topic in public while simultaneously trying to solve a mystery. Things continued downhill as I floundered. The audience's bad reaction intensified into a solid wall of Boo! Boo! Boo! And I still couldn't figure out what I had done wrong.

Then I noticed that my cat Boo was behind me on the live video. My audience knows Boo, and they were happily calling out her name. They weren't booing me so much as totally ignoring me in favor of a cat they had never met. Still, that was better than getting booed.

My point is that context matters. If you don't know the whole story, you can't always tell the difference between getting booed off the stage and watching people try to communicate with a cat using the written word. They can look the same.

Probably the single biggest error that humans make in their decision-making is ignoring relevant context. Sometimes we do it intentionally, as in avoiding news and information sources that would give a competing explanation of reality. That problem can be fixed simply by broadening your information sources. But a bigger problem comes from not knowing what you don't know.

Think of all the times you had a firm opinion about some topic in the news, only to later learn you didn't have the full story. It's common. I'm not exaggerating when I say it happened to me about five times this week alone. The initial news reports indicated that someone had done

something terrible, and within a day or so I learned—after more context had been added to the story—that my first impressions were completely wrong.

That's why I like to wait two days before forming a strong opinion
on events in the news. The initial reporting is so often wrong or out of
context that it's a waste of energy to immediately get worked up about
what you see in the news. Just wait a few days, and there's a high likelihood you will learn the catastrophe that was reported was no big deal
once you hear the context. Or the thing that looked minor is actually a
catastrophe. It works both ways.

In October 2018, the New York Times published a timeline about how
the slogan #JobsNotMobs was created by a user on Twitter and caught
on so well that it became part of President Trump's rally speeches and
tweets. The Times reported my involvement in that chain of events
this way:

> Scott Adams, the creator of the "Dilbert" cartoon strip, quickly
> endorsed "jobs not mobs" as a potential slogan. Because of the
> cartoonist's popularity among the pro-Trump crowd online, this
> was a key moment.

It is true that my Twitter account, with more than 324,000 followers at this writing, includes a lot of pro-Trump folks. But an important
bit of context is missing to make sense of this story. I'm also famous
among people who follow politics for writing about the topic of persuasion, which includes my New York Times bestselling book Win Bigly, my
popular blog posts on Dilbert.com, and my daily Periscope livestreams
that are monitored by most of the large media sites as well as the White
House, or so I have been informed. So when I endorsed the slogan as
powerful, people familiar with my persuasion talents correctly believed

"jobs not mobs" had a lot of persuasive power, and that was what caused them to put energy behind it. Here's how I endorsed it in my tweet. I was commenting on Ali Alexander's tweet discussion of the word mobs.

@SCOTTADAMSSAYS

"Mobs" by itself doesn't work. But "Jobs Not Mobs" is brain glue plus framing and contrast. Science says the brain interprets rhymes as persuasive.

The New York Times[1] story indicated that my contribution was a function of my popularity with the target audience. That account lacks the key context that I'm famous among Twitter users who follow Trump-related politics for my understanding of this specific topic: political persuasion. I'm a trained hypnotist, and I have studied persuasion in all its forms for decades as part of my talent stack for being a writer. The main theme of my persuasion content is that President Trump has weapons-grade persuasion skills, and so, by my view of the world, it is no accident the president and I both saw the persuasive power of #JobsNotMobs. Almost any trained persuader would see it immediately.

If you follow politics, you know the news media outlets that are the least friendly to President Trump, including the New York Times, don't often describe him as having useful skills. In this case, they had to leave out the context of my persuasion skills, and the president's too, in order to tell the story without accidentally complimenting either of us for having a valuable talent. By omitting context, the Times turned a story about persuasion talent into a story about popularity. If you were not aware of the context, you would not know anything was missing.

People who are often the subject of news and articles, such as me, know that perhaps 60 percent of the time the reporting is either completely wrong or lacks important context that would change your opinion of the situation. If, during the course of this book, you find yourself thinking I am far too distrustful of experts, the media, and people in general, you have to understand my context. If you see a story about a stranger, you usually can't tell how accurate it is. But when I see a story about me, I know exactly what they get wrong. The same is true for nearly every negative story you hear about me on the Internet. I know the various scandalous stories about me are fake because I know what context they leave out. But you can't tell. As I said, my best guess is that the news about me is wrong or misleading about 60 percent of the time. And the mistakes are not always harmless. I've seen published stories about me that claim I'm part of the Alt-Right, a Holocaust-denier, and the creator of *Garfield*. None of those things are true, but at least two of them could get me into a bar fight if someone believed them.

My assumption is that negative stories about other public figures, and other major issues in the news, are similarly wrong or misleading. Here's a good rule of thumb.

Reports about famous people and other newsworthy topics are either wrong or misleading about 60 percent of the time, often because they lack context. Wait a few days before forming an opinion on anything new, just in case context is missing. It usually is.

LISTENING TO THE EXPERTS

I don't recommend ignoring experts, no matter the field. But sometimes you will need to violate the advice of experts to accomplish anything meaningful. I'll give you some examples.

In 1988, while still working my corporate job at the local phone company, I tried to become a cartoonist in my spare time. I submitted samples of my work to the major syndication companies that sell comics to newspapers all over the world. Four of the companies receiving my samples, staffed by the top experts in the world on the commercial value of comic strips, rejected me. One syndication company said yes. Dilbert went on to become one of the most successful comic properties of all time. Four out of five experts were wrong about my potential.

I used to be an expert myself. When I worked for my local phone company, my job was to predict the costs and benefits of financial decisions over three to five years. My estimates were approximately as accurate as what one might expect from a squirrel with a spreadsheet. I was an expert, and I was almost always terribly wrong. In my defense, people who do financial predictions on complicated situations are wrong most of the time. And when they are right, it is luck.

We live in a world in which it is dangerous to ignore the advice of experts, but it is almost as dangerous to follow their advice. The trick is to know when the experts are the solution and when they are the jailers of your mental prison.

I find it most useful to believe experts when the situation is simple and there is some historical situation much like it. In those cases, experts have a good handle on what works and what doesn't. But for situations in which there is overwhelming complexity, there is no historical pattern that is predictive, and experts disagree, treat that sort of expert opinion as no more useful than an educated guess.

FAKE NEWS FILTER

One of the most useful systems I have developed for understanding the world involves routinely flipping back and forth between CNN and Fox News coverage. When I encounter someone who is stuck in either one of the two silos, left or right, I can quickly recognize the situation because they lack awareness of the argument on the other side. It is one thing to disagree with an opposing viewpoint, but it is a far bigger problem if you have never heard it. And that is a common situation in American politics.

Recently I asked a prominent Democrat if he was aware that smart people such as Bill Gates believe modern nuclear technology—specifically the Gen IV plants that are safe from meltdowns and eat nuclear waste from other sites as their fuel—are the most promising path for dealing with the risk of climate change. He said he was unaware of it, and he didn't think others in his political peer group were aware of it either. For many Democrats, the risk of climate change is seen as catastrophic, and yet their news silo prevents too many of them from being aware of the most promising way to address it. Stories without proper context are a dangerous type of fake news, and often the hardest to spot. Here are some tips on identifying potential fake news.

Four-Point Check: News that is true will generally be reported the same on right-leaning news sites Fox News and Breitbart, as well as on left-leaning CNN and MSNBC. If they all say a hurricane is heading your way, pack your bags. If only the right-leaning news sites or only the left-leaning news outlets report something as fact, it probably isn't.

Team Bias: The "side" that is out of power is more likely to generate fake news. When President Obama was in office, Fox News told you he was destroying the country in a thousand ways. CNN was a bit more balanced about President Obama, and more likely to talk of his accomplishments. Under President Trump, CNN pivoted to nonstop negativity about Trump's performance, and Fox News became more of a cheerleader. The news outlet whose political side is out of power does the most fearmongering because that's what sells to their viewers. The side that has its preferred president in power has the advantage of being able to point to some accomplishments over time, even if they have to exaggerate to do so.

Mind Reading: Look for signs that news pundits are reading the minds of politicians to find problems. That usually means things are not as bad as the headlines suggest. The news business needs a full pipeline of news—preferably the bad kind—to feed their business model. If all they can find to complain about is their own opinion about the unspoken thoughts of strangers, the world is in a good place.

Doom Predictions: Look for signs that the reported bad news is really a prediction of doom from someone who is a political partisan. Predictions of doom from cheerleaders for one team or another are almost always exaggerated.

Manufactured Outrages: Look for signs that pundits are actively misinterpreting, or taking out of context, someone's comments that would have been no big scandal without the devious sleight of hand.

Absurdity: If you see news that is so absurd it is literally unbelievable, that's usually because it isn't true. The old saying in the news business is that a dog biting a man is not news, but a man biting a dog is. It would be highly unusual for a man to bite a dog, but one could imagine it happening in our crazy world. So that doesn't qualify as absurd, just unlikely. The absurd case would be a story about a pet cemetery located near a nuclear waste site that reanimated a dead dog that went on to bite someone.

Fog of War: For breaking news, don't believe the first quotes you hear, the body counts, the implications for the future, whose fault it is, or much else about the story until some of the noise settles down. Experience tells us that the initial reports on most things are inaccurate.

News that is reported the same by news outlets on both the left and the right is probably true. If you only see a story reported by news sites that lean in one direction, it probably isn't true.

PERSUASION

As I have mentioned too often, when I was in my twenties, I took an evening class to learn to be a hypnotist. That launched me on a decades-long quest to better understand how the human mind works, with a special interest in learning how to persuade. The most important thing one learns as a hypnotist is that people are not fundamentally rational when it comes to many of life's biggest questions. Instead, we are a species that makes one irrational decision after another and then we cover our tracks by concocting "reasons" after the fact. In other words, we are not so much a rational species as a species that experiences the illusion of being rational. If you don't understand that basic quality of human nature, you will be trapped forever in your mental prison. Your persistent belief in your own rationality is the primary illusion that controls your life. Once you learn to see past that illusion, the walls of your mental prison will start to melt away.

If people were rational, you would observe that they changed their opinions on topics such as religion and politics when presented with new information that contradicts existing beliefs. But we don't see anything like that, at least not commonly. Instead, we see people ignoring facts, imagining things that don't exist, accusing the other team of bad character, believing coincidences mean more than they do, and generally acting irrationally no matter what facts are in evidence.

We humans can be rational about the little stuff, when we have no emotional investment. But most of what we care about has plenty of emotion, including your romance, family, career, religion, politics, lifestyle, and even hobbies. Irrationality dominates our important decisions, but it is generally wearing a rational disguise that you unwittingly provide.

If you want to understand the world as it is, instead of the myth of human rationality, any one of these books will set you free. I recommend reading them in this order:

Influence—by Robert Cialdini
The Power of Habit—by Charles Duhigg
Thinking, Fast and Slow—by Daniel Kahneman
Win Bigly—by Scott Adams

For more reading on the same topic, do an Internet search on "persuasion reading list" to see my own recommendations, which I sometimes update.

> If you think humans are rational about their biggest priorities, you are poorly equipped to navigate life.

MANAGING EMBARRASSMENT

Earlier in this book, I told you it is more effective to think of your ego as a tool than it is to think of it as who you are. But that is easier said than done. Our egos control us through fear, and often that fear is an illusion. Here are the two key exercises you can use over your lifetime to keep your ego from being your jailer.

> Put yourself in potentially embarrassing situations on a regular basis just to maintain practice. If you get embarrassed as planned, watch how one year later you are still alive. Maybe you even have a funny story because of it.

And . . .

> Note how other people's embarrassments mean little to you when you are an observer. That's how much your embarrassments mean to them: nothing.

Using those two techniques, I have evolved from being embarrassed about just about everything to having almost no sense of shame whatsoever. Like most things in life, practice matters. If you practice controlling your ego, you can learn to do it effectively over time. It doesn't happen overnight, but if you work at it, you'll see big gains in a year. And the gains will accumulate.

CHANGE WHAT YOU DO TO
CHANGE HOW YOU THINK

Your brain makes decisions and causes your body to do whatever it is you decide to do. But it also works the other way, and that is an important tool for escaping your mental prisons. You can change how you think by changing what your body is doing.

In the simplest example, if you travel and talk to people from different cultures, the relocation of your body helps a great deal to expand your mind.

You have probably noticed how radically your mood and your thoughts can change after exercise, eating, and even having sex. And if you don't get enough sleep, you know your thoughts take a different path than if you did. One of the most important conceptual shifts you can make is the realization that you can program your thoughts and your attitudes by taking care of your health and fitness.

How many times have you considered a challenge and decided it was too overwhelming to take on because you were tired, hungry, or physically weak? And how many times have you noticed that being in good health with lots of energy persuades you to take on bigger challenges and more risks of nonlethal embarrassment? I'm describing most of you. If you want to think more effectively, make sure you manage your body in a way that gets you there. Learn to eat right and exercise right. Treat sleep as a learned skill. Those topics are beyond the scope of this book, but you would do well to read my book *How to Fail at Almost Everything and Still Win Big* to learn how to create simple systems to get all of that done.

To think more effectively, improve your fitness, diet, and sleeping.

JUDGING THE MISTAKE VERSUS THE RESPONSE

If you're similar to most people, you judge others by whatever mistakes you believe they have made. I was the same way for much of my life. But I eventually realized it was a form of loserthink. A smarter way of thinking is to judge people by how they respond to their mistakes.

I'm sure that's the standard you would like applied to your own bad choices in life. We all make mistakes, and I consider that a permanent feature of being human. But how we handle ourselves once the mistakes occur is a better standard for judging each other.

One big problem with judging people by their mistakes is that what you are actually doing is judging people by the mistakes you are aware of. The people you have judged to be angels might simply be better, or luckier, at getting away with their transgressions against humanity. That would result in an inaccurate ranking of human beings on your personal judgment scale. There's no point in being a judgmental person if you can't accurately rank people. That's just guessing.

Another problem with judging people by their mistakes is that we make mistakes too, and we always have "reasons" for ours. Sometimes we think you haven't seen the full picture. Sometimes we are tired, dumb, frightened, angry, or otherwise off our games when we make decisions, and those moments do not represent the person we are most of the time. Sometimes we think our mistakes were not mistakes at all, even if it looks that way to others. Sometimes we are blamed for things we didn't do. Sometimes we have different priorities, so perhaps the thing you thought was a mistake was the thing I thought was in the interest of the greater good. And so on. The point is that civilization works best when the standard of acceptable behavior that you want applied to you is the same one you apply to others. You could call that a subset of the Golden Rule: Do unto others as you would have them do unto you.

We humans are judgmental people, and we can't turn off that feature of our brains. Nor would we want to do so, since judging our environment is what keeps us alive. Consciousness is a continuous loop of looking for patterns and problems and judging them so we know what to do next. You can't turn off your judging any more than a planet can turn off its own gravity. But what you *can* do is make a decision to judge people's lesser transgressions by how they respond to their mistakes, as opposed to judging the mistakes. I find that approach to be the most useful way of judging people. If you try it for a year, you'll have a hard time going back to the old hypocritical way of judging people by their mistakes—a standard you would not like applied to you.

Just to be clear, society at large has to judge people's mistakes in the context of the legal system. You can't forgive a crime in a legal sense, or else society would come apart. And when choosing employees, friends, or lovers, it is entirely sensible to assume that whatever patterns you've observed in people's past actions are more likely to continue than to suddenly stop. I don't propose ignoring clear patterns of behavior.

What I do recommend is that we judge the character of others by how they *respond* to their mistakes, whenever that is practical. And the best response a person can make to a mistake follows this pattern:

1. Fully acknowledge the mistake and its impact.
2. Display genuine-looking remorse.
3. Explain what you plan to do to make amends.
4. Explain how you plan to avoid similar mistakes.

If you do those four things, I'm likely to come away from the experience thinking you are better than most people I've encountered despite your original mistake. That is a productive way of thinking for both the judger and the judgee, in the sense that society works better if we embrace that standard.

Most of the people in my part of the world have been informed by their religions to hate the sin but not the sinner. But that is hard to do because it is so counter to the way our brains are wired that we prefer outsourcing the task of forgiving to a deity. My proposed standard of judging people by how they respond to their mistakes allows you to keep your god out of it and still get a good outcome.

Judging people by their response to mistakes, as opposed to the mistakes alone, will allow you to feel better about your own mistakes, as long as your response follows the four steps. We humans like to have clear rules of behavior, and the four steps are clear. Follow the steps and you can feel better about yourself and better about others. It will make the world a kinder and less confusing place.

THE FORTY-EIGHT-HOUR RULE AND THE TWENTY-YEAR RULE

Have you ever wondered where the rules of etiquette come from? I mean, who was the first person to suggest saying "Bless you" to sneezers? Who decided that holding the elevator door is polite whereas pretending you don't see someone running toward the elevator while you repeatedly pound the Close button is not polite?

Someone has to invent new rules of etiquette every now and then to keep up with the changing times. I have invented two new rules that I recommend adopting because doing so will make the world a better place. On top of that, these new rules allow you to avoid loserthink.

The Forty-Eight-Hour Rule

The Forty-Eight-Hour Rule says that everyone deserves forty-eight hours to clarify, apologize for, or otherwise update an offending statement. The clock starts when the offender first realizes people are taking offense.

Until the two-day period has passed, my proposed rule of etiquette is that observers can state how it makes them feel and can politely ask for a clarification. But it is impolite to assume you correctly interpreted an offending statement. Once the clarification/apology/update is offered, you are free under this standard to express your opinion of it.

If you don't immediately see the value of the Forty-Eight-Hour Rule, you probably don't follow the news. About half of all news coverage involves taking people out of context, acting offended, and creating hours of content out of nothing but sarcasm.

As a public figure, I have often wished the Forty-Eight-Hour Rule existed. Strangers attack me on social media several times a day for things they only imagine I think, said, or did. Rarely do my critics *actually disagree* with me, which I know sounds strange to those of you who live your lives in private. But after directly observing literally thousands of criticisms of my public opinions on a range of topics over the years, I can tell you that no more than 10 percent of those criticisms involve an accurate interpretation of my opinions or the context in which they were made.

When you feel offended by someone else's statement, make it a habit to wait forty-eight hours. You'll be surprised how often you've misinterpreted the message. And that's not a coincidence. While it is somewhat rare for people to intentionally say outrageously offensive things in public, it is extraordinarily common for people to be misinterpreted. The Forty-Eight-Hour Rule gives people the benefit of the doubt consistent with the odds.

It is loserthink to imagine you can accurately discern the intentions of public strangers. It is better to ask people to clarify their opinions and accept that as the best evidence of their inner thoughts.

As a practical matter, the only way we can navigate life is by continuously making assumptions about the intentions of others. I'm not suggesting you can turn off that instinct. But the most productive—and reasonable—way to respond to an offensive statement is to wait for the clarification or apology. And that is because most offensive statements are not what they seem at first glance. Once you have better context and more reliable facts, you're on more solid ground to act as if you understand the offender's point and intention. And even then, you're often wrong. But at least you can say you tried to be open-minded. We don't live in a society where people can be open-minded as much as we might like. But it makes the world a better place if we are conspicuously trying.

In 2018, Roseanne Barr posted a career-crippling tweet that was widely criticized for sounding racist. She tweeted that former Obama advisor Valerie Jarrett looked like what you would get if the Muslim Brotherhood and *Planet of the Apes* had a baby. That's a funny line if you have seen Valerie Jarrett's haircut, and you know the character played by white actress Helena Bonham Carter in *Planet of the Apes*, and—this is the crucial part—you are unaware that Jarrett is part African-American. Roseanne claimed she was unaware of that fact. Personally, I wouldn't have guessed it either, based on Jarrett's looks.

When critics tore into Roseanne for her alleged racist tweet, she immediately denied it had racist intent. I found her denial credible: what public figure would *intentionally* compare an African-American to an ape, in public, and think it would all work out? Even an actual racist wouldn't do something that dumb, assuming they also starred in a hit television show. To me, it isn't a credible accusation that Roseanne's tweet had a racist intent.

When analyzing this sort of situation, I have the advantage of having "famous-person perspective." I've experienced one publication after another accusing me of all sorts of heinous intentions I know to be false while readers assume they are true. Nonfamous people know that *sometimes* the press distorts what famous people say. But they generally don't know how common it is.

Adding to the credibility of my interpretation of Roseanne's intentions is that she clarified she didn't mean it as a race comment, and she appeared to be consistently and emotionally horrified that anyone would interpret it that way.

Still, I'm no mind reader. I could be wrong. I have been wrong before. But what I can say with 100 percent certainty is that Roseanne's critics are not mind readers either. We're all looking at the clues and making assumptions about her inner thoughts.

The Roseanne situation is what caused me to suggest the Forty-Eight-Hour Rule for public clarifications. The rule, if followed, would allow anyone to clarify a statement that has been interpreted negatively. Once the clarification is given, I think the press and the public should accept the clarification.

But wait, you say—what if the clarification is nothing but an ass-covering lie?

The Forty-Eight-Hour Rule suggests you should accept the lie as if it were the truth, then move on. That's how a lot of social interactions work. We call it "manners."

YOUR FRIEND: Sorry I'm so late. Traffic was terrible!

YOU (THINKING): *That's probably a lie.*

YOU (TALKING): Glad you got here safely! Let me buy you a drink.

We can't be the thought police. It isn't a practical way to run a society. But it is both practical and useful to insist that people *do and say* the right things. If you have evil thoughts, but consistently do and say things that are good for the world, you're a good person in my book.

Shorter version: You are what you do, not what you think.

Likewise, if you harbor some bigoted thoughts, but you have managed to use your sense of reason to override them and act in ways society approves, I'm good with you too. I won't judge you by your thoughts. But I will certainly let you know if your actions (including your words) work against the greater good.

Part of my thinking on this topic is influenced by the fact that people evolve to become whatever they say they are. If a bigot says in public often enough that racism is evil, the bigot is self-influencing himself to be less racist. We are better off encouraging insincere but positive opinions, because they are self-fulfilling to a degree. Reward what works. If you are getting the right actions, something is working, and it puts people on the path of faking it until it becomes real. I'll take that situation over guessing what people are thinking and condemning them for it. We can't have a successful culture based on condemning people for presumed thoughts.

When you see someone clarify an "unbelievable" story into something totally ordinary, you can usually trust that the ordinary version is the correct one. I won't claim this works every time, but it is rarely a good idea to believe the unbelievable when the alternative is to believe the ordinary.

When you see an "unbelievable" story in the press that is based on interpreting someone else's meaning, it is generally fake news. Wait for the clarification to see if there is a perfectly ordinary explanation.

The Twenty-Year Rule

Let's stop blaming each other for things that happened more than twenty years ago. Humans change a lot in two decades. If we are lucky enough to mature and learn over time, we become better versions of our younger selves—wiser, less selfish, and more useful.

In olden times—let's say, before the Internet—your mistakes of youth would go unrecorded. The Twenty-Year Rule applied by default in most cases, because no one had an efficient way to check up on your behavior that far back.

Now we have social media that creates a total slideshow of every dumbass thing you ever thought or did in your entire life. It turns out that most of us were worse people when we were younger. You wouldn't want to know the teenage me. But I'd like to think I've improved since then. I'll agree to judge you by your most recent twenty years on this planet if you will extend me the same courtesy.

I realize this isn't a perfect system. Some of us have done things in our past so awful that no time can forgive. But the alternative is worse. If you can judge me today by what I did fifty years ago, I can do the same with you. That way leads to darkness.

If social media didn't exist, the Twenty-Year Rule would be less urgent. But we are perilously close to judging each other by our worst decisions in high school. That's no way to organize society.

> It is loserthink to judge people by their much younger selves.
> People change. And they usually improve.

CONSPIRACY THEORIES AND HOW
TO KNOW YOU FELL FOR ONE

If you are engaged in discussing politics, you have probably accused others of falling for conspiracy theories. There's a good chance others have accused you of the same thing. So how can you figure out who is in the mental prison and who is the wise observer from the outside? I'll give you some tips on doing just that.

There Are No Experts on Your Side

It is fairly common for experts to disagree on big issues, even when 95 percent are on one side. It is far less common for 100 percent of the experts to be on the same side while the other side is comprised entirely of non-experts. For example, there are no trained astronomers who believe the earth is flat. If you are unable to find one credible expert working in the right field to agree with you, maybe it's time to rethink your belief.

Invisible Elephant in the Room

Hallucinations generally involve adding imaginary things to the environment. For example, if you think you see ghosts, UFOs, or Bigfoot, you are imagining them added to the existing scenery. What you rarely or never see is a hallucination that subtracts something from the existing reality. For example, you never hear of people hallucinating that the furniture in their homes is missing when it is actually still there right in front of their eyes. So if you and other people are looking at the same evidence in the same place at the same time, and you can clearly see something the rest do not see, the problem is probably on your end. Here I am not talking about *interpretations* of data. I'm talking about seeing something as clearly as the hand in front of your face. If you see it, and others cannot, bet on the people who *don't* see it, because hallucinations are usually additions to reality, not subtractions.

HOW TO KNOW IF YOU ARE IN A CULT

If you are a member of a cult, your leader is probably telling you crazy things and expecting you to believe them. For example, if your leader is telling you to kill yourself so you can free your soul to live for eternity beneath a couch cushion, you might want to skip the next meeting. But simply knowing that cults peddle falsehoods won't help you determine if you are in a cult, because the press, politicians, spiritual leaders (except yours, of course), and special-interest groups are brainwashing the public with falsehoods all the time. Your favorite news source is almost certainly doing as much brainwashing as informing, but you probably think that sort of thing only happens to the sad bastards who make the mistake of consuming the wrong news sources.

No one is exempt from society's powerful brainwashing forces. The press is telling its viewers what they want to hear—one version of reality for the political right and one version for the left—and it looks exactly like truth to the respective audiences. If you're human, confirmation bias and what you believe to be your "common sense" are identical in how they make you feel. That's why I often say you can't look at the past, or even the present, to know the truth about your reality, because it is easy to fit different theories to the same set of observations.

If you want to test the validity of your worldview, it isn't good enough that the facts in evidence are consistent with your theory of events. Multiple theories can meet that standard. *The only practical way to test your worldview is to see how well it predicts.* If you belong to a group whose interpretation of reality does a good job of explaining the past (or so it seems) yet is bad at predicting the near future, you are probably in a cult, or something that acts like one.

As I write this chapter, the United States is grappling with several different interpretations of reality around the same set of observed facts: was President Trump a Russian asset, or did the so-called Deep State try to frame him? Both theories fit the observed facts available to the public. Constitutional law professor Jonathan Turley has suggested a third theory for consideration: that both sides of the topic are experiencing confirmation bias, and there was neither Russian collusion nor Deep State conspiracy, just a lot of people believing in conspiracy theories. If you are keeping score at home, that makes three entirely different realities that all conform to the facts in evidence, at least according to the adherents of each.[2] Obviously, most of the players in this drama believe that the people who disagree with them have the wrong interpretation of the facts. Perhaps by the time you read this book, we will know which reality won out.

If you have a preferred religious belief, keep in mind that billions of people practice other religions and they believe *you* are the one in the cult while they are the enlightened ones. My point is that knowing cults brainwash their members won't help you determine if you are in one. Brainwashing wouldn't work if you knew it was happening to you. For the average person, confirmation bias will convince you that your group is the one that has life figured out while everyone else is flailing blindly.

And that perception will almost certainly be an illusion. Once you learn to embrace the realization that being right and being wrong feel exactly the same, you're halfway out of your mental prison.

> **Being absolutely right and being spectacularly wrong feel exactly the same.**

The clearest signal you're in a cult is that other members of the group actively try to prevent you from exchanging ideas with outsiders. For example, Democrats and Republicans increasingly avoid the company of the other, and the smart ones avoid talking politics in mixed company because it rarely ends well. One could make an argument that both Democrats and Republicans are evolving from whatever they once were to something closer to accidental cults that worship their preferred news sources and adopt the opinions assigned to them.

For the past several years, I have been writing about American politics using what I call a *persuasion filter*. Through that work, and the interesting people I have recently met, I have learned things about the true nature of reality that are so startling you wouldn't believe me if I told you. We can test that assumption because I'm going to tell you right now: there are only about a dozen people in the United States—perhaps six on the political right and six on the left—who decide what the public thinks about politics. That small group routinely influences how the news is framed, and the rest of the pundits simply amplify the messages and brainwash the public through repetition. I'm sure you have noticed the sameness in how pundits handle their respective narratives on the left and the right. None of that is an accident. A handful of influencers create the framing for stories, the pundits amplify, and the public believes.

If you believe the news you consume is organic and unbiased, you might be less of an informed citizen than an accidental member of a cult, but without the bad haircut requirement.

If your view of reality is consistent with the past but fails to do a good job predicting the near future, you might be in a cultlike organization with a manufactured worldview. If members of your group discourage you from listening to opposing views, it's time to plan your escape.

CHAPTER 14

How to Break Others Out of Their Mental Prisons

O nce you learn to break out of your own mental prison, you might feel generous enough to help others do the same. I will teach you some techniques to do just that.

If you have ever tried to win a debate by providing better facts and reasoning, you know it almost never works. That's because people are confident in their own abilities to understand the world. That confidence should be your target, not the totality of the argument. Rarely can you free someone from mental prison in one try. You will need to chip away at their sense of confidence about their opinions first, to weaken the prison walls until they can punch their way out on their own.

People who have studied psychology and persuasion are already primed to know they can be confident and wrong at the same time. But almost everyone else thinks their sense of confidence is a good indicator of how right they are. Maybe they have never noticed the high levels of confidence coming from the people who totally disagree with them.

Confidence is not a reliable signal of rightness, at least not when it comes to the big political and social questions. We generally observe high levels of confidence from opposite positions on every issue. To help people out of their mental prisons, first you must train them to stop trusting their understanding of the world.

If you have ever found yourself in a debate online, you know it usually goes like this:

YOU: The grass in my lawn is green.

CRITIC: This idiot thinks polar bears can fly!!! LOL!

YOU: I never said anything remotely like that.

CRITIC: Then explain what you meant when you wrote, "The grass in my lawn is green."

YOU: That has nothing to do with polar bears.

CRITIC: That's what you want us to believe, but the overlap in the context of the larger media narrative is conflating your near-term bias to be larger than the whole.

Once your critic starts spouting word-salad nonsense like that, it is a sign of cognitive dissonance, and it means your critic's argument has fallen apart. But it probably won't help you much, because your critic will also be declaring victory based on the fact that you "refused to address his criticism."

In my experience, perhaps 90 percent of the people who think they are disagreeing with me are only disagreeing with their own misinterpretation of my opinion. When you find yourself in a similar situation, as I am sure you sometimes do, I recommend using something I call the Magic Question.

THE MAGIC QUESTION

The most effective approach to addressing critics who misinterpret you, and then criticize their own misinterpretation as if it came from you, is this challenge:

State ONE thing you believe on this topic that you think I do NOT believe.

I've been testing this question on social media for a year, and it works great. If you let your critic focus on his hallucinations about your opinion, you will get nowhere. But if you change the focus to the critic's opinion, it puts you in control of the conversation. In other words, you flip the conversation from artificial disagreement, in which your critic imagines crazy opinions for you and then debunks them, to one in which the critic is stating his opinion and you are agreeing. That process looks like this, in an exaggerated form:

CRITIC: You think a border wall is the only solution to immigration! LOL! You must be a racist or an idiot.

YOU: State ONE thing on the topic of border control that you think is true and you believe I do not.

CRITIC: Well, for example, you think we need a wall for every inch of the border.

YOU: I don't think that. I think we only need a wall where it makes sense functionally and economically. We are in total agreement.

CRITIC: Well, you also believe a border wall will stop all drugs! LOL!

YOU: I don't believe a border wall will stop all drugs. We are in complete agreement.

You might have to repeat this process, one point after another, until your critics lose their confidence in their ability to read your mind and discern your opinions. By itself, this technique will not bring down a prison wall. But it can weaken the structure.

When people have solid evidence to back their opinions, they generally lead with the strongest evidence and downplay the rest. But when people are experiencing cognitive dissonance and confirmation bias (which is our normal human state), they tend to use what I call *laundry list persuasion*. That happens when none of the evidence is persuasive on its own, so there is an attempt to make up for the shortfall with quantity. The idea here is that if one piece of evidence has zero credibility, ten pieces of evidence with zero credibility add up to something real. That, of course, is nonsense to an objective observer, but keep in mind we are talking about people trapped in mental prisons, not rational actors.

In my experience, if someone has up to three reasons for an opinion, that person might have a strong case. But people who present laundry lists of ten reasons rarely have a strong case. I can't say this rule of thumb is predictive every time, but you can easily test the validity of a person's laundry list with this request: *Give me the strongest argument or evidence on your list that supports your point. Just one, please.*

Your critic will usually smell a trap, resist your request, and demand that you consider all the damning evidence on the laundry list. Here's how to reply: *In the interest of time, would you agree that if I can debunk your strongest point, you should rethink all of your points that are weaker than the one I debunk?*

If you can't debunk the strongest point, you might be the one in the mental prison in this case. But if you can, I don't recommend debunking anything else on the list, even if you have the time and desire.

Remember, your goal is to reduce the other person's confidence in their rightness. Taking their strongest argument off the table (if you can) should be enough to get that done. Don't get lost in the weeds of the smaller points on the laundry list. Debunk the strongest point according to your critic, declare the rest of the arguments to be weaker than the one you debunked, and call it a day. If you do your job right, your targets will have less confidence in their opinions and over time it could help them punch their way through their lesser illusions.

Don't play Whac-A-Mole with people who have laundry lists of reasons supporting their hallucinations. Ask for their strongest point only, and debunk it if you can. Target their undue confidence, not their entire laundry list.

PACING

This isn't a book on persuasion, but the concept of pacing is important for breaking people out of their mental prisons. Pacing involves matching the person you hope to persuade by agreeing with as much of their position as you can without lying, in order to build rapport and trust before taking on the disagreements. Always talk first about the points on which you agree, to set the tone and establish yourself as a reasonable voice.

If you are debating a topic in the news, I find it helpful to start by noting that all news sources are unreliable at least sometimes. Most people will agree with that as a general statement. Once you have established that high-ground truth, you have set the table for persuasion. Remember, your objective is to weaken the other person's confidence in their sources of information, and in so doing weaken the walls of their mental prison.

> Agree with people as much as you can without lying, and you will be in a better position to persuade.

DEFINE THE WEEDS

One of the ways people lock themselves in mental prisons is by not differentiating between the things that matter and the things that do not. I blame the news and social media for that, because unimportant news can often be the most entertaining and most profitable. Our human instinct is to assume that whatever subject we think about the most must also be the most important. That is backward, of course, because we should be picking the most important topics to think about the most. The business model of the news industry and the design of social media almost guarantee we will be thinking the most about the least important topics. Your news sources can get more clicks about a political gaffe or a hypocritical opinion than they can from chattering about the boring details of a new law or discussing a disaster that was skillfully avoided.

Despite our collective addiction to unimportant news, most people can easily recognize what is important and what is "in the weeds" of triviality, but often it has to be pointed out and framed like this:

CRITIC: Your favorite politician said something offensive today.

YOU: That is true, but trivial compared to the economy and national defense, both of which are stronger than ever.

The losing approach here is to debate whether or not the politician was as offensive as claimed. It is more effective to accept minor criticisms while framing them as relatively unimportant. Here again, the objective is to persuade your critics that they are not good at sorting out what matters from what is in the weeds. You are not trying to change their minds outright.

> Don't argue in the weeds of a debate. Dismiss the trivial stuff and concentrate on the variables that matter. That gives you the high ground.

DESCRIBE THE LONG TERM

I often find myself in online debates with people who have a good grasp of the short-term trade-offs of a decision but they overlook the long-term picture. When that happens to you, rather than pointing out the omission, ask your critic to describe what the future would look like under their preferred plan. If they struggle to do so, it will weaken their confidence in their opinion.

If your critics can describe a long-term future that looks good for their preferred paths but you disagree, your best move is to suggest looking for a way to test your competing ideas small before committing to something long term. You won't always have that option, but in many situations you will.

> Ask people with opposing opinions to describe what the future would look like if their view of the world were to play out. Does it sound reasonable?

CALL OUT THE MIND READING

In an earlier chapter, I talked about how often we assume (incorrectly) that we can read the minds of others. I have observed over the past few years that when I point out that someone is forming an opinion based on what they believe to be their ability to read minds, they will often drop their confidence levels right away. If it doesn't happen immediately after you cleverly label their behavior as mind reading, try this next: ask how many times in their personal relationships their mates or friends have incorrectly assumed what they were thinking. This approach hits people hard. We all know it is common for the people who know us best to misinterpret our thoughts and intentions. So what are the odds we can accurately deduce the inner thoughts and intentions of total strangers?

Once you have established with your critic the idea that mind reading is absurd, and they flail around for a bit to defend how good they are at it, you have already weakened their confidence. None of us are good at mind reading, and we know it, even if we don't admit it.

Once you have introduced the mind reading criticism, people will be primed to notice it, and the idea will grow in power over time. I know that to be true because my followers on social media throw it in my face every time I cross the subtle line from judging people by their actions to judging them by what I assume are their intentions. It's a sticky idea.

This is as good a place as any to remind you that I make almost every loserthink mistake in this book, and routinely. But I am also sure I am reducing my rate of loserthink over time simply because I focus on it. I expect you will have the same experience after reading this book.

The best way to avoid the mind reading illusion is to look for it in others. That will prime you to better catch yourself when you do your own mind reading.

FRAMING ISSUES

If you ask the wrong question, you usually get the wrong answer. The same is true for how you frame an issue. If you frame it correctly, you have a better chance of understanding it and dealing with it effectively. In the world of politics, partisans frame things for selfish gain, not for solutions.

As I write this, the president of the United States is asking for funding to build a "wall" on the border with Mexico, while the Democratic Congress is insisting we need some fences, sure, but not walls. The problem is framed in political terms as opposed to useful terms.

A more useful way to frame this situation is to point out that politicians shouldn't be making engineering decisions. They should set the specifications, approve a starter budget, and let border experts and engineers decide what they need to build and where. I suggested such a framing in a tweet on December 14, 2018, in which I wrote, "Politicians shouldn't be making engineering decisions. Approve the border control budget and let a panel of engineers decide how much is wall and how much is other. #Engineers."

Once you see this framing, you realize the only thing stopping the government from funding an effective border upgrade is that they framed the problem as political and the public let them get away with it. It was always an engineering decision, working with the border security experts to understand the problem and its requirements.

Most of the other big issues in the country have the problem of bad framing. Democrats want the government to be a productive part of getting healthcare to citizens, but Republicans frame that as socialism versus capitalism. That political framing makes progress nearly impossible.

On the other side, Republicans want effective border control, and Democrats frame that as a case of good versus evil (mostly racism). That political framing makes progress nearly impossible too.

Democrats frame climate change as a case of wise scientists versus moronic science-deniers. Republicans frame climate change as a case of gullible simpletons who fall for junk science versus wise businesspeople who can see it is a scam. Neither framing is productive. A better frame is to see climate change risks as something the public needs to understand better so we're all on the same side, wherever that leads.

Bad frames never produce good solutions. If you see someone locked in a mental jail because of a wrong frame, sometimes you can help by suggesting a more productive frame. There is no simple rule for finding the right frame, but in my experience everyone recognizes a better frame when they see it. So brainstorm framing options until one stands out as more productive, and test it with a few people to make sure they see it the same.

You can't get the right answer until you frame the question correctly. And partisans rarely do.

CHAPTER 15

A Final Word

I f you made it all the way to the end of this book, you are well on your
way to leaving your mental prison behind. It might happen quickly, or
it might take some time. Now that you have been exposed to the productive thinking techniques in this book, you will start to notice them
in your environment, and that will reinforce your understanding of
them and move them closer to the top of your mind.

I'll say one more time that I have made every mistake in this book,
usually more than once. If you follow me on Twitter, at @ScottAdams
Says, you'll see me making some of these mistakes again, but you will
also see people correcting me. That delights me and helps me at the
same time. But it never embarrasses me.

Moving toward the Golden Age is a joint project. It requires all of
us to think more productively and to nudge each other as needed. Collectively, I hope we can lose our superstition about "common sense"
and replace it with the time-tested ways of thinking that are spread
across different disciplines and summarized in this book.

Science tells us that people retain only a small part of what they learn, so I will close by telling you which parts you should try hardest to remember.

THINGS TO REMEMBER

- Don't engage in mind reading. It isn't a human skill.
- Think of your ego as a tool, not your identity. Track your predictions to build up some useful humility about your worldview. Put yourself in embarrassing situations regularly to teach yourself there is no lasting pain.
- The past no longer exists. Don't let your attachment to the past influence your decisions today.
- If you haven't mentioned the next best alternative to your proposed plan, you haven't said anything at all, and smart people would be wise to ignore you.
- If you are arguing over the definition of a word instead of the best way forward, you are not part of the productive world.
- If you are sure one variable is all you need to grasp a complicated topic, the problem is probably on your end.
- Occam's razor (the idea that the simplest explanation is usually correct) is utter nonsense in the way it is commonly employed. We all think our opinions are the simplest explanations.
- Fairness cannot be obtained in most cases because of its subjective nature. The closest you can get is equal application of the law.
- If your argument depends on that one time something happened, you do not have an argument. You have a story.
- If your argument depends entirely on the so-called slippery slope, you don't have much of an argument. Everything

changes until there's a reason for it to stop. Mowing your lawn is not a slippery slope to shaving your dog.

- Coincidences usually mean nothing. And they are the fuel of confirmation bias. If your argument depends entirely on not knowing how else to explain coincidences, you have a poor imagination, not an argument. Coincidences might tell you where to look first for confirmation of a theory, but that is as far as they can go.
- Avoid halfpinions that ignore either the costs or the benefits of a plan.
- Don't use analogies to predict. Look to causes and effects.
- Don't judge a group by its worst 5 percent. If you do, you're probably in the worst 5 percent of your own group.
- Understand the limits of expert advice, and be skeptical of experts who have financial incentives to mislead.

Those are the most powerful points to take away, but I hope you find value in the rest of the book as well and refer to it often. I also hope you find a reason to gift it to someone in your life who could benefit from more productive ways of thinking.

Thank you for reading my book!

Acknowledgments

Thank you to the social media trolls who made this book possible. If it had not been for your nonstop attempts to make me sad, I would not have had the material to write this book. Nor would it have been this much fun.

Thank you to all the people in my life who have pointed out the flaws in my thinking over the years. I didn't like it when it was happening, but I have learned to recognize it as a gift. I tried to pay it forward.

Thank you to my amazing editor, Leah Trouwborst, for helping me engineer this book. You impress me with your talent and professionalism, and I'm hard to impress.

Thank you to my publisher, Adrian Zackheim, for giving me the confidence to become an author years ago, and for continuing to trust my voice on completely different topics. Your trust makes me do better work.

Thank you to Zora DeGrandpre for checking my science references in this book. If I got anything wrong in my interpretation of the science, don't blame her; she probably told me not to write it that way. Sometimes I chose simplicity over completeness, to convey the general point without getting lost in the weeds.

Thank you to Kristina Basham for accepting and loving me exactly the way I am. You are the best part of my life.

Notes

CHAPTER 1: WHAT IS LOSERTHINK?

1. K. Mahmood, "Do People Overestimate Their Information Literacy Skills? A Systematic Review of Empirical Evidence on the Dunning-Kruger Effect," *Communications in Information Literacy*, 2016, 198–213.
2. Aaron E. Carroll, "Peer Review: The Worst Way to Judge Research, Except for All the Others," *New York Times*, November 5, 2018, www.nytimes.com/2018/11/05/upshot/peer-review-the-worst-way-to-judge-research -except-for-all-the-others.html.
3. Sheila Kaplan, "Duke University to Pay $112.5 Million to Settle Claims of Research Misconduct," *New York Times*, March 25, 2019, www.nytimes.com/2019/03/25/science/duke-settlement-research.html.
4. Richard Jacoby, "The FDA's Phony Nutrition Science: How Big Food and Agriculture Trumps Real Science— and Why the Government Allows It," *Salon*, April 10, 2015, www.salon.com/2015/04/12/the_fdas_phony _nutrition_science_how_big_food_and_agriculture_trumps_real_science_and_why_the_government _allows_it/.
5. Dan Robitzski, "Faulty Studies Mean Everything You Know about Nutrition Is Wrong," *Futurism*, July 2018, https://futurism.com/the-things-we-know-about-nutrition-are-wrong-thanks-to-faulty-studies; Julia Bel- luz, "Why (Almost) Everything You Know about Food Is Wrong," *Vox*, August 16, 2016, www.vox.com /2016/1/14/10760622/nutrition-science-complicated.
6. Susan Solomon and Diane J. Ivy, "Emergence of Healing in the Antarctic Ozone Layer," *Science*, July 15, 2016, 269–74.
7. Einstein Sabrina Stierwalt, "Why Is the Ozone Hole Shrinking?," *Scientific American*, March 22, 2017, www .scientificamerican.com/article/why-is-the-ozone-hole-shrinking.

CHAPTER 3: THINKING LIKE A PSYCHOLOGIST

1. Julia Jacobs, "DeSantis Warns Florida Not to 'Monkey This Up,' and Many Hear a Racist Dog Whistle," *New York Times*, August 29, 2018, www.nytimes.com/2018/08/29/us/politics/desantis-monkey-up-gillum .html.
2. Marc Fisher, John Woodrow Cox, and Peter Hermann, "Pizzagate: From Rumor, to Hashtag, to Gunfire in D.C.," *Washington Post*, December 6, 2016, www.washingtonpost.com/local/pizzagate-from-rumor-to -hashtag-to-gunfire-in-dc/2016/12/06/4c7def50-bbd4-11e6-94ac-3d324840106c_story.html.

NOTES

3. Jean Kumagai, "Finally, a Likely Explanation for the 'Sonic Weapon' Used at the U.S. Embassy in Cuba," IEEE Spectrum, March 1, 2018, https://spectrum.ieee.org/semiconductors/devices/finally-a-likely-explanation -for-the-sonic-weapon-used-at-the-us-embassy-in-cuba; Julian Borger, "Mass Hysteria May Explain 'Sonic Attacks' in Cuba, Say Top Neurologists," *The Guardian*, October 12, 2017, www.theguardian.com/world /2017/oct/12/cuba-mass-hysteria-sonic-attacks-neurologists.
4. L. Trick, E. Watkins, S. Windeatt, and C. Dickens, "The Association of Perseverative Negative Thinking with Depression, Anxiety and Emotional Distress in People with Long-Term Conditions: A Systematic Review," *Journal of Psychosomatic Research*, December 1, 2016, 89–101; F. Clancy, A. Prestwich, L. Caperon, and D. B. O'Connor, "Perseverative Cognition and Health Behaviors: A Systematic Review and Meta-Analysis," *Frontiers in Human Neuroscience*, November 8, 2016, 534.
5. "Chronic Stress Puts Your Health at Risk," Mayo Clinic, March 19, 2019, www.mayoclinic.org/healthy -lifestyle/stress-management/in-depth/stress/art-20046037.

CHAPTER 5: THINKING LIKE AN HISTORIAN

1. Michael H. Romanowski, "Problems of Bias in History Textbooks," *Point of View*, March 1996, 170–73; Ray Raphael, "Are U.S. History Textbooks Still Full of Lies and Half-Truths?," History News Network, https:// historynewsnetwork.org/article/7219.

CHAPTER 6: THINKING LIKE AN ENGINEER

1. "Overdose Death Rates," National Institute on Drug Abuse, January 29, 2019, www.drugabuse.gov/related -topics/trends-statistics/overdose-death-rates.
2. Dan Braha and Marcus A. M. De Aguiar, "Voting Contagion: Modeling and Analysis of a Century of U.S. Presidential Elections," *PLOS ONE*, May 18, 2017, DOI:10.1371/journal.pone.0177970.

CHAPTER 7: THINKING LIKE A LEADER

1. J. J. Halpern and R. C. Stern, eds. *Debating Rationality: Nonrational Aspects of Organizational Decision Making* (Ithaca, NY: Cornell University Press, 1998).

CHAPTER 8: THINKING LIKE A SCIENTIST

1. Lewis Johnson, "Searching for the World's Best Investments? Begin by 'Inverting,'" July 26, 2018, http:// blog.capitalwealthadvisors.com/trends-tail-risks/searching-for-the-worlds-best-investments-begin -by-inverting.
2. Charles T. Munger, *Poor Charlie's Almanack: The Wit and Wisdom of Charles T. Munger*, 3rd ed., (Marceline, MO: Walsworth, 2005).

CHAPTER 9: THINKING LIKE AN ENTREPRENEUR

1. Glenn Kessler, "Do Nine out of 10 New Businesses Fail, as Rand Paul Claims?," *Washington Post*, January 27, 2014, www.washingtonpost.com/news/fact-checker/wp/2014/01/27/do-9-out-of-10-new-businesses-fail-as -rand-paul-claims/?utm_term=.edc51535420f.

CHAPTER 10: THINKING LIKE AN ECONOMIST

1. Shoshana Zuboff, *The Age of Surveillance Capitalism: The Fight for a Human Future at the New Frontier of Power* (New York: Public Affairs, 2019).

NOTES

2. Robert J. Szczerba, "15 Worst Tech Predictions of All Time," *Forbes*, January 9, 2015, www.forbes.com/sites /robertszczerba/2015/01/05/15-worst-tech-predictions-of-all-time/#75e002531299.

3. "25 Famous Predictions That Were Proven to Be Horribly Wrong," List25, March 13, 2014, https://list25 .com/25-famous-predictions-that-were-proven-to-be-horribly-wrong/5/.

4. "Things People Said: Bad Predictions," www.rinkworks.com/said/predictions.shtml.

5. Allison Berry, "Top 10 Failed Predictions," *Time*, October 21, 2011, http://content.time.com/time/specials /packages/article/0,28804,2097462_2097456_2097459,00.html.

6. "25 Famous Predictions That Were Proven to Be Horribly Wrong," List25, March 13, 2014, https://list25 .com/25-famous-predictions-that-were-proven-to-be-horribly-wrong/.

CHAPTER 11: THINGS PUNDITS SAY THAT YOU SHOULD NOT COPY

1. Olivia Beavers, "Jimmy Carter: Media 'Harder' on Trump Than Other Presidents," *The Hill*, October 22, 2017, https://thehill.com/homenews/administration/356639-carter-media-has-been-harder-on-trump-than -other-presidents.

2. B. S. McEwen, "In Pursuit of Resilience: Stress, Epigenetics, and Brain Plasticity," *Annals of the New York Academy of Sciences*, February 25, 2016, 56–64; J. A. Sturgeon, P. H. Finan, and A. J. Zautra, "Affective Disturbance in Rheumatoid Arthritis: Psychological and Disease-Related Pathways," *Nature Reviews Rheumatology*, September 12, 2016, 532–44.

CHAPTER 12: THE GOLDEN AGE FILTER

1. "25 Famous Predictions That Were Proven to Be Horribly Wrong," List25, March 13, 2014, https://list25 .com/25-famous-predictions-that-were-proven-to-be-horribly-wrong/5/.

2. Taylor Hatmaker, "A Popular Genealogy Website Just Helped Solve a Serial Killer Cold Case in Oregon," TechCrunch, January 31, 2019, https://techcrunch.com/2019/01/31/hlavka-murder-gedmatch-dna/; Alex Horton, "A Suspected Killer Eluded Capture for 25 Years. Then Investigators Got His Aunt's DNA," *Washington Post*, February 17, 2019, www.washingtonpost.com/crime-law/2019/02/16/suspected-killer-eluded-capture -years-then-investigators-got-his-aunts-dna/?utm_term=.6d643569909a.

3. Steven Beard, "Is There Really Evidence for a Decline of War?," OEF Research, May 8, 2018, https://oefresearch .org/think-peace/evidence-decline-war.

4. "Yemen Crisis: Why Is There a War?," BBC News, March 21, 2019, www.bbc.com/news/world-middle-east -29319423.

5. "10 Breakthrough Technologies 2019, Curated by Bill Gates," *MIT Technology Review*, February 28, 2019, www.technologyreview.com/lists/technologies/2019/.

6. "Secretary Perry Launches Versatile Test Reactor Project to Modernize Nuclear Research and Development Infrastructure," Just the Real News, March 2, 2019, www.justtherealnews.com/2019/02/28/secretary -perry-launches-versatile-test-reactor-project-to-modernize-nuclear-research-and-development -infrastructure/.

7. Ibid.

8. Climeworks, 2019, www.climeworks.com.

9. Valeria Perasso, "Turning Carbon Dioxide into Rock—Forever," BBC News, May 18, 2018, www.bbc.co.uk /news/world-43789527.

10. Global Thermostat, 2019, https://globalthermostat.com.

11. Strata Worldwide, 2019, www.strataworldwide.com.

12. WhenHub, 2019, www.whenhub.com.

13. Mandy Roth, "4 Ways Telemedicine Is Changing Healthcare," Health Leaders, August 28, 2018, www .healthleadersmedia.com/innovation/4-ways-telemedicine-changing-healthcare.

14. "Better Health with Smartphone Apps," Harvard Health, April 2015, www.health.harvard.edu/staying-healthy/better-health-with-smartphone-apps.

15. Angelica LaVito, Christina Farr, and Hugh Son, "Amazon's Joint Health-Care Venture Finally Has a Name: Haven," CNBC, March 6, 2019, www.cnbc.com/2019/03/06/amazon-jp-morgan-berkshire-hathaway-health-care-venture-named-haven.html.

CHAPTER 13: HOW TO BREAK OUT OF YOUR MENTAL PRISON

1. Keith Collins and Kevin Roose, "Tracing a Meme from the Internet's Fringe to a Republican Slogan," New York Times, November 4, 2018, www.nytimes.com/interactive/2018/11/04/technology/jobs-not-mobs.html.

2. Jonathan Turley, "Witch Hunt or Mole Hunt? Times Bombshell Blows Up All Theories," The Hill, January 12, 2019, https://thehill.com/opinion/judiciary/425033-witch-hunt-or-mole-hunt-times-bombshell-blows-up-all-theories.

Index

Note: Page numbers in *italics* refer to illustrations.

239

INDEX

INDEX

mind reading
  calling out, 227–28
  illusion of, 24–32, 231
  and intentions of others, 212–13
  and moral equivalency arguments, 142–43
  in the press, 202
  of Reiner, 34
misinterpretations, challenging, 221–24
mistakes
  judging responses to, 207–9
  as learning experiences, 39, 70, 192–93
  refusing to admit to, 147
mockery, 3–4, 18, 79–80
money
  allocating across multiple risks, 134–36
  made from bad behavior, 122–23
  motivating power of, 120
  paired with complexity, 13–14, 85
  time value of, 132–34
moral equivalency, 141–42
MRI scanners, 182
MSNBC, 201
Munger, Charlie, 101
Musk, Elon, 4

naming things, power of, 3, 4–5
Native Americans, 60–61
negative, proving a, 103–4
negative terms, employing, 4–5
negativity, 46–51, 158
Nest, 136
news programming. See press
Newsweek, 84
New York Times, 9–10, 197–98
"normalizing," 145–46
North Korea, 70
nuclear power, Generation IV, 174, 179, 201
nuclear powers, 169–70
nutrition science, 14–15

Obama, Barack, 65, 202
Ocasio-Cortez, Alexandria, 109, 150–51, 151
Occam's razor, 32–33, 231
offensive statements, 210–14
Olsen, Ken, 138
one-variable illusion, 83–86, 231
opinion stacking, 21
opioid addiction crisis, 81
opposite outcomes, considering, 101–2
optimism, 158–59
ordinary vs. extraordinary explanations, 29, 30
outrage, manufactured, 202
ozone hole predictions, 15

Pastis, Stephan, 41
pattern recognition of humans, 66–70, 150–52
peace, 168–72

peer-reviewed studies, 9–10
performance as related to self-worth, 43–45
Periscope posts of author, 42, 58, 193, 197
Perry, Rick, 178
personal control, 111–14
persuasion
  author's skill set in, 18, 197–98, 203
  book recommendations, 204
  compromised by need to be right, 42–43
  and fairness arguments, 148–49
  and hyperbole vs. legitimate opinions, 90
  and illusion of rationality, 203–4
  laundry list persuasion, 223–24
  as leadership skill, 87
  and pacing, 224–25
  and prediction models in climate science, 16
  use of patterns/analogies in, 150–53
Pizzagate conspiracy theory, 29
political arguments, 42–43, 148
political candidates, verbal gaffes of, 26–29
political commentary career of author, 42, 93,
  189, 193
political warming, 22–23
politicians, fact checking claims of, 89
population size, 139, 164
positivity, 50–52, 158
posture, 36, 37, 38
poverty, 163–64
The Power of Habit (Duhigg), 204
praise, power of, 161
predictions about the future
  and Adams Law of Slow-Moving Disasters, 139
  based on analogies/patterns, 151–53, 232
  based on causation, 151–52
  based on entrepreneurial energies, 139–40
  and climate change, 16, 172
  and complexity paired with money, 13–14
  and creative panic, 15
  discarding of failed predictions, 12–13
  of doom, 202
  for finances/investments, 8–9, 133
  and "history repeats" premise, 67–73
  keeping track of your incorrect, 39, 231
  as means of testing worldviews, 217, 219
  necessity of, 16
  as persuasion, 16
  by the press, 202
  and scam models, 12–13
  and science, 8, 8, 12, 13, 15, 16
  straight-line, 137–40
presidential election of 2016, 84–85
presidents and job performance polling, 128–30
press
  and ability to measure audience reactions,
  21–22
  absurdity in, 202–3
  and anecdotal evidence, 100

243

For more game-changing life hacks and penetrating analysis of our political moment, check out Scott Adams's other books:

PORTFOLIO
PENGUIN